Cooking With the Spices of India

COOKING WITH THE SPICES OF

India

50 Easy to Follow Recipes to Transform Ordinary Foods Into Extraordinary Meals

INTRODUCTION BY KATHLEEN O'ROURKE

◆

RECIPES BY

KATHLEEN O'ROURKE & JULIA SCANNELL

Published by
Culinary Alchemy, Inc.
Post Office Box 393
Palo Alto, California
94302
1.800.424.0005
Manufactured in the United States.

Contributing Editors: Elizabeth Connolly & Julia Scannell

Design by Elizabeth Ives Manwaring
San Francisco, California

ISBN 0-9647724-0-X

First Edition

FOR SHARABI KABABIS EVERYWHERE!

◆

MANY THANKS TO THE INCREDIBLE PEOPLE WHO MADE THIS WORK
POSSIBLE THROUGH SHARED KNOWLEDGE, EMOTIONAL SUPPORT,
RECIPE TESTING, DESIGNING AND EDITING.

ELIZABETH CONNOLLY
ELIZABETH IVES MANWARING
KURIAN & JOSEPH THOMAS

AND OUR TASTERS EXTRAORDINAIRE

MARY O'ROURKE, KEVIN PRUESSNER
& JACK SHERIDAN

About the Recipes

All the recipes, meat, vegetable and grain, in this book are grouped in proportions advised by the United States Food and Drug Administration's "Food Pyramid." Sweets and meats are recommended in small amounts, while the foundation of the diet is based on grains, fruits and vegetables. ◆ This type of diet has been proven to reduce the risk of heart disease, diabetes (a common problem in our aging population) and even cancers, such as colon cancer. Weight control and simply feeling energized and clear-headed are additional benefits to people of all ages. ◆ At times, the recipes in this book use oil, and even butter or cream. When used in moderation, these fats are flavorful and do not cause harm. In contrast to many styles of cooking, we do not use fats or salts as an obligatory source of flavor. Spices and herbs plus the recipe's main ingredients, such as the vegetable or meat, are the main sources of flavor. However, if you, or someone you are cooking for, has a health problem requiring very low amounts of fat, skip the few recipes that require more fat than a little cooking oil, and try the many flavorful sautés and baked dishes. Cut even more oil from the recipes by using water or wine to finish cooking a dish after starting with a reduced amount of oil. A non-stick skillet and a watchful eye will prevent the mixture from drying out and burning.

About Culinary Alchemy

Culinary Alchemy was founded on the principle that busy people have been doomed to uninteresting and even unhealthy food for too long. The lack of time in most of our lives makes it hard to pursue new interests in foods, especially those from faraway places with ingredients that are unfamiliar. Our products are collections of the freshest ingredients for authentic ethnic cooking. Ingredients are identified and paired with unadulterated cultural recipes. People who live or have lived in areas uncompromised by faster ways of eating retain the secrets of their ancestors in food preparation and flavor combinations. We always emphasize recipes that embody the intelligence of a country's home chefs. The results are exquisite meals with flavors that ring true. For more information on our products, call 1.800.424.0005.

Contents

Introduction

KATHLEEN O'ROURKE

IT HARDLY SEEMS POSSIBLE TO TELL THE STORY OF INDIAN CUISINE. ITS INGREDIENTS, ITS GENERATIONS OF HOME COOKS AND THEIR RECIPES, ALONG WITH THE LEGACY OF PARSI, JEWISH, PORTUGUESE, ANGLO AND, OF COURSE, MUGHAL INVADERS AND SETTLERS, ALL COMBINE TO FORM A KALEIDOSCOPIC ARRAY OF TRADITIONAL EATING. THE CUISINE'S DIMENSION KNOWS NO BOUNDS. AND THE INTELLIGENCE OF ITS INGREDIENT COMBINATIONS, WHICH BEGAN 4,000 YEARS AGO, HAS EVOLVED INTO A FINE ART.

In the United States, the popularity of Indian food has been slow to evolve. Somehow the rich variety of the food has been reduced to a single term: "curry." Indian food is not curry powder, which originated as an English concoction, and it is not soupy, yellow mixtures. Instead, it is a cuisine that expertly uses spice as an accent to enhance the intrinsic flavors of fresh ingredients.

Over 900 million individuals populate the country of India. Their physical characteristics, languages and foods all vary according to region and religion. In the north, Indian dishes bear the influence of the bygone Mughal courts. This northern food is characterized by dishes such as biryani, a pilaf of basmati rice with meats or vegetables, slow-cooked lamb dishes and recipes featuring a comforting and aromatic thick sauce. It is these dishes, with the thick sauce or gravy, that Indians refer to as curry—simply, a dish with sauce. In the southern states of India, dishes such as *idlis*, *dosai* and *sambar* feature uniquely southern spice combinations, like sambar powder. In the east, the Bengalis are known as fish eaters and have numerous recipes for seafood using their spice mixtures, such as *panch phoran*. In the eastern state of Hyderabad, agriculturally renowned for chili production, the food is especially hot.

Although the food of each region may be different, in every case the spicing for the dishes is worked out on an individual basis by the chef according to family custom and personal taste. To a true Indian cook, using a standard "curry" powder would be an unthinkable way to prepare a dish. Each day, spices are toasted and ground fresh in an Indian home. The preparation process releases aroma and removes bitterness.

A properly prepared Indian meal uses spice to create an incomparably tantalizing display of color, aroma and flavor. In the west, there is a tendency to overspice food when attempting an Indian recipe. It is hard for us to believe that spice measured out to $1/8$, or even $1/16$, of a teaspoon can impact the flavor of a dish. Indian cooking reflects the wisdom of using spice to accent foods, not overwhelm them. By learning how to cook Indian dishes, we learn how to use spice. This knowledge transfers to everyday cooking and gives an option to flavoring food with traditional European ingredients: fats, creams and salt.

Good Living

"I DO NOT DRINK WHILE WALKING.
I DO NOT EAT WHILE LAUGHING—SO HOW
CAN I BE A FOOL, OLD MAN?"

This proverb may sound a little silly to us, but it is an ayurvedic teaching remarking on what used to be conventional wisdom. That is, when a meal is taken, other activities stop and everyone sits down to enjoy eating. Today it seems more people are eating not only while walking, but actually while running.

Whether it's fast food or home-made, a good portion of our day is spent procuring food. The activity is too comprehensive and important to our lives to ignore the quality of the food we are eating. Eating at nice restaurants doesn't really help in the quest to eat well and healthily. Fat is a quick, economical and easy way to flavor a dish. More dishes than you probably want to know about contain too much fat. The only way to have truly interesting, nutritious food at a good price is to learn how to cook it yourself.

The other benefits of cooking in the home become obvious as you share your creations with friends and family. There is no greater act of generosity than preparing a well thought-out meal for others. The result is a warm and relaxed gathering with shared laughter and new memories.

Using Whole Spices

The recipes in this book teach how to cook with whole spices. And no, learning how to work with whole spices is not equivalent to learning how to make water from scratch! To get good flavor and aroma, grinding and toasting your own spices is worth the extra effort. Similar to coffee beans, whole spices retain the strength of their essential oils better than ground spices, because ground spices have a large surface area, in proportion to their granule size, exposed to air and damaging light. Additionally, pre-ground spices purchased at the store are likely to originate from low quality seeds. By freshly grinding spices, you are better able to control their quality.

To keep spices their freshest, protect them from light, particularly fluorescent light, and store them in a cool area. Clear glass or plastic jars are poor storage containers for aromatic seeds. Finally, make sure to use your ground spices within three months, and whole spices within six months or a year.

Spice Preparation

The first rule of thumb to abide by when preparing spices is not to use them raw. The second is never use burned spices—throw them out and start over.

Raw spices taste bitter and are problematic to digest. The two ways to prepare them for use are *tarka* and toasting. A *tarka* is done by heating oil in a skillet over medium-high heat, adding the whole seeds and allowing them to sputter, or pop in the case of brown mustard seeds, for about 30 seconds. Afterwards, the other ingredients in the recipe are added.

The second technique is toasting, or dry roasting. A dry skillet is heated over medium-high heat and the spices are added. Occasionally swirl the spices or perform a flipping motion to prevent burning. The spices take a couple of minutes to become fragrant, and in the case of cumin, an incense-like smoke rises from the seeds. Set the spices aside to cool, then either store them whole or grind them. In some cases, a recipe will call for two different items to be toasted, which can be done together.

Spices & Aromatic Seeds

The flavors and aromas of spice are extremely difficult to describe in words. Each spice and aromatic seed lends its own characteristic properties to a prepared dish. The way to know a spice is to use it, and thus become familiar with the flavors and quantities that are appropriate to combine in a dish. In India, the spices are used so subtly that a favorite pastime is guessing what spices are included in a dish. Each cook has a secret spice signature that confounds all who eat her meals. The following descriptions will help you start expertly combining flavors.

Ajwain Seeds

Lovage is another, perhaps more familiar, name for ajwain. The spice is indigenous to southern India, and has a thyme-like pungency. Ajwain is one of the hard-to-find spices that is generally edited out of cookbooks in the United States due to unavailability. However, ajwain is commonly used in India and gives a distinctive note to fish and starchy vegetable dishes. Use it slightly crushed.

Amchoor

Dried green mango slices are sometimes used whole in India, but most recipes call for the spice in its powdered form, called amchoor. India cultivates many varieties of mango. Some are best when ripened to full sweetness and others are picked green and made into pickles. Green mangoes are also used for amchoor powder. Crumble the spice well before adding it to a dish.

Asafetida

In Latin, *fetida* means stinking, and it is the most obvious characteristic of this resinous spice. Asafetida, or *hing* in Hindi, is obtained from the rhizomes of the giant fennel plant. It can be purchased in a pure, brown block or as a powder, which ranges in color from brown to yellow. The recipes in this book were developed using yellow *hing*. Asafetida is credited with the prevention of flatulence, and is used with beans and starchy vegetables. You may recognize its onion-like flavor from the *papadams* served in Indian restaurants.

Bay Leaves

There are different varieties of bay leaves around the world. The Turkish bay leaf is mild, and the one used in Indian cookery. The California bay leaf is generally used in Mexican cookery, and has a strong scent and flavor. Either can be used, just be aware of the differences. The bay leaf adds depth to stews, pilafs and any number of starchy, slow-cooked dishes. To use the leaves, tear them into several large pieces—the torn edge is what imparts the flavor.

Black Peppercorns

Black pepper has always been the king of spice. Most of the world's early exploration resulted from the quest for black pepper. Prior to the arrival of this spice from India, Europeans had been doomed to a listless diet flavored by mustard and salt.

Black peppercorns are the sun-dried, fermented green berries from the pepper vine. The less pungent white pepper is processed black pepper, useful for light-colored sauces. Pink peppercorns are *schinus molle* and are unrelated to pepper. While universal in its use, black pepper is often treated too harshly for its fragile nature. Heat and air are extremely damaging to black pepper's volatile oils, so it should be freshly ground and added to a dish at the end of its cooking time. If you don't own a pepper grinder for the kitchen, you should.

Cardamom Pods & Seeds

Cardamom is the vanilla of India. Used in savory stews and sweets, it has a wonderful complex, sweet flavor. Cardamom is a member of the ginger family and it grows on the hills of the Malabar coast. For better freshness, the spice should be purchased in whole green pod form. White cardamom pods are bleached green pods, a process damaging to essential oils! The green pods are used whole or ground with the husk. Or, the seeds are removed from the husk and ground.

Cayenne

A variety of chilies are used to make cayenne, so this powder varies in heat and color, as well as coarseness of grind. Cayenne, whole dried hot red chilies and green chilies are the only sources of intense heat in an Indian dish. Most of the recipes in this book give a range of quantity to add to the recipe, depending on personal heat preference: mild to hot, but not scorching.

Chili Peppers

Chilies originated in Mexico and were introduced to the rest of the world by European explorers. Over time, the chili has become an integral part of many cuisines, including Chinese, Indonesian and Thai. Whole dried hot red chilies are frequently used in Indian cooking. They are generally 2-3 inches long, and supply flavor as well as heat. The chili is often toasted, which mellows its flavor and removes bitterness. The *tarka* method is even more common for tempering chilies in India (see page 11). Keep in mind that chilies impart heat to a dish over time. Make sure they are removed before serving, or tell your guests not to eat them.

Cinnamon

Cinnamon quills are rolled from the bark of the cinnamon tree, a member of the laurel family. Many spice companies sell cassia, a relative of cinnamon, which has very hard and dark quills. True cinnamon originated in Ceylon, now Sri Lanka. Ceylon cinnamon is a lighter brown color and has a light, almost lemony flavor. It is easily broken into pieces.

Cloves

Cloves are unopened flower buds from an evergreen tree. Their name comes from the Latin word *clavus*, meaning nails. In India, cloves have such a high level of essential oil, they can actually be lit on fire. Cloves impart a very powerful flavor, and should be used only in small amounts lest their flavor dominate a dish.

Coriander Seeds

Grown all over the world, coriander has much subtle variation in flavor, color and size. When toasted, coriander fills the nose with a warm soft fragrance. Indian coriander is the most fragrant and flavorful, with large, lemon-colored seeds. Moroccan coriander has small, dark seeds and is the most prevalent variety in grocery stores. It is best used in pickling, not cooking. Egyptian and Canadian coriander are the best substitutes for the Indian variety.

Cumin Seeds

Used the world over, cumin is one of the principal spices of Indian cooking. It has a strong aroma and flavor, and can be quite bitter if the seeds are not toasted or cooked in some manner. Cumin is used whole or ground, and is found in all sorts of vegetable, fish and meat recipes.

Cumin Seeds, Black

Shahi jeera, or kingly cumin, is black cumin. This spice is often confused with kalonji and caraway, even by Persians and Indians, whose recipes call for it. Black cumin is closely related to cumin, and actually looks like a very dark cumin seed with consumption and a crick in its back—sort of curled and thin. The spice is cultivated in Kashmir and is difficult to find in the west. The flavor of black cumin is superlative, lending a smoky nature to a dish.

Fennel Seeds

Fennel is from the anise family and is often used as a breath freshener in India. The type for cooking and the type used as the after-dinner mint are actually different varieties. One of the most common western uses for fennel is in sausage. The whole seeds have a wonderful impact on the flavor of *kebabs* and *koftas*, which are the Indian ground meat preparations most similar to sausage.

Fenugreek Seeds

Fenugreek is a peculiar square-shaped, very dense spice. The seeds are used in tiny amounts, five or six seeds per dish in most cases. Fenugreek has a strong flavor and should be toasted to remove bitterness. The seeds can also be germinated into high-protein sprouts that make a great addition to salads.

Kalonji

This tear-shaped, coal-black spice is often mistakenly referred to as black cumin or caraway by Persian cooks. The confusion intensifies when you consider the western names for the spice are nigella and black onion seeds. Kalonji is in no way related to the onion. This spice is often edited out of recipes due to its rarity, but adds a welcome pungency and flavor to many breads and other recipes.

Mace

(SEE NUTMEG)

Mustard Seeds, Brown

Mustard seeds come in three varieties: yellow, brown and black. By and large, when black is called for, brown mustard seeds are what is meant. Black mustard seeds have a coarse flavor compared to brown mustard seeds. The less pungent yellow mustard seeds are best for pickling and are rarely used in Indian cooking. Mustard seeds must be popped in hot oil or ground to release their flavor.

Nutmeg & Mace

The nutmeg tree produces a round fruit, but the item of interest is the fruit's pit. When cut open, the fruit shows a brown nugget with a mesh of thick, red strands wrapped around it. These strands are called mace, and they turn golden in color as they dry and age. The nugget in the center has a thin shell, which reveals the nutmeg when cracked. Nutmeg is used in all sorts of dishes around the world: baked goods, meats, and even mashed potatoes in the Netherlands. The more potent mace is used in a similar fashion, but in lesser quantity. Nutmeg's flavor is much better when freshly ground.

Turmeric

In a land where color, aroma and flavor are all important to a satisfying meal, turmeric is the major source of color in many dishes. A pinch of the deep yellow powder brightens the color of vegetables and meats alike. Of course, turmeric should not be used in a way that drenches a whole meal in yellow. Instead, as with the other spices, it should be used in moderation, to accent the natural color and disposition of the main ingredient in the dish. Turmeric is a root that is related to and resembles fresh ginger. When fresh, turmeric is bright orange, and is prized medicinally for its antiseptic qualities.

Urad Dal

Urad dal is the split and hulled gram bean. The recipes in this book generally use this legume as a spice—that is, it is used in small amounts to flavor oil with its peanut-like taste before other ingredients are added to the skillet.

Spice Blends

MASALAS

Masala means mixture, and all Indian dishes take advantage of masalas for their flavoring. A masala may consist of dried spices, herbs, onion and garlic. Each element may be added in succession during the entire preparation period and it is still referred to as the masala, or mixture, of the dish. Some masalas are preground and added to a dish all at once. There are as many masalas as there are cooks in India. Each household has its mixtures according to family preferences.

The following recipes are for the masalas used in this book. Make them fresh and store in an airtight container out of direct light. The fresh aroma and flavor of the ground blends will be their most potent in the first three months.

Garam Masala is the classic masala of north India. Garam means warm and is an ayurvedic reference to the spices in this recipe. The blend is not only hot to taste, but it is internally warming to the body and therefore should be avoided in the very hot months of India's summer.

YIELDS APPROXIMATELY 3 TABLESPOONS

1/3 whole nutmeg
1 1/2 teaspoons cardamom seeds
1 1/2 teaspoons black peppercorns
1 1/2 teaspoons black cumin seeds
1 1/2 teaspoons coriander seeds
A 2-inch stick cinnamon
1/2 teaspoon whole cloves
A curl of mace

Break the nutmeg into pieces by firmly knocking it with the bottom of a coffee mug. Put all the masala ingredients in a medium skillet. Toast the spices over medium-high heat, swirling the skillet occasionally, until they become fragrant, about 3-5 minutes. Let the spices cool slightly, transfer them to a spice/coffee grinder and pulse the switch to pulverize them into a fine powder. Transfer the mixture to a storage container.

SHAHI MASALA

This Gujarati-style masala is one of our favorites—it has incredible depth in its fragrance. When mixed with yogurt, it can be used as a marinade for almost anything. For one example, see Tandoori-Style Chicken (page 90).

YIELDS APPROXIMATELY 3 TABLESPOONS

12 whole green cardamom pods
1/8 teaspoon cardamom seeds (seeds from approximately 5 green cardamom pods)
1 1/2 teaspoons black peppercorns
1 teaspoon coriander seeds
2 dried hot red chilies
1 teaspoon fennel seeds
A large pinch ajwain seeds
A large pinch ground asafetida
1 teaspoon turmeric

Put all the masala ingredients, except the asafetida and turmeric, in a medium skillet. Toast the spices over medium-high heat, swirling the skillet occasionally, until they become fragrant, about 3-5 minutes. Let the spices cool slightly, transfer them to a spice/coffee grinder and pulse the switch to pulverize them into a fine powder. Empty the powder into a small bowl and mix in the asafetida and turmeric. Transfer the blend to a storage container.

PANCH PHORAN

Panch Phoran is the distinctive flavoring combination of Bengal and is used whole. A dish using the blend is generally started with a *tarka* to infuse its signature flavor into oil.

YIELDS 5 TEASPOONS

1 teaspoon fenugreek seeds
1 teaspoon kalonji seeds
1 teaspoon cumin seeds
1 teaspoon fennel seeds
1 teaspoon brown mustard seeds

Mix all spices in a jar and shake well. Always give the blend a shake before using, as the mustard seeds have a tendency to drop to the bottom of the jar.

SAMBAR POWDER

This south Indian mixture is used in sambar, a type of vegetable soup (see Radish Lentil Soup, page 30), braised dishes and lentil broths. Usually the mixture is made with a high proportion of dried hot red chilies and, as expected, is a scorching blend. This particular recipe has been toned down. It has fantastic flavor, but if intense heat is desired, simply add more cayenne or red chilies.

YIELDS APPROXIMATELY 4 1/2 TABLESPOONS

2 tablespoons coriander seeds
3/8 teaspoon cumin seeds
1/8 teaspoon fenugreek seeds
4 dried hot red chilies
1 teaspoon black peppercorns
3/8 teaspoon urad dal
3/8 teaspoon moong dal
1 1/2 tablespoons turmeric

1/2 teaspoon ground asafetida

Put the coriander, cumin, fenugreek, chilies and black peppercorns into a large skillet. Toast the spices over medium-high heat, swirling the skillet occasionally, until they become fragrant, about 3-5 minutes. Let the spices cool slightly and transfer the spices to a spice/coffee grinder. In the same hot skillet, toast the urad dal and moong dal over medium-high heat until slightly browned, about 2-3 minutes. Let the dal cool, add to the spice/coffee grinder and pulse the switch to pulverize the mixture into a fine powder. Empty the powder into a small bowl and mix in the turmeric and asafetida. Transfer the blend to a storage container.

Special Ingredients

CLARIFIED BUTTER
Ghee

Ghee is truly a divine ambrosia! In India, ghee has been a religious offering for centuries. After smelling it, it is easy to understand why the gods would find it remarkable. For those newly arrived to the Indian culinary world, ghee is also known as French brown butter. Vegetable oil or butter can be used as substitutes in a pinch. But, I highly recommend that you give yourself the ghee experience.

YIELDS 3/4 CUP

2 sticks unsalted butter (equal to 1 cup)

Place the butter in a very small saucepan and completely melt over very low heat. Melting will take about 5 minutes. Raise the heat to low and simmer the butter until the gurgling becomes sporadic, about 10-15 minutes. At this point, the milk solids on the bottom of the pan will start to brown. Allow them to do this for about 5 minutes, but don't let them burn! Remove the pan from the heat and let cool. Skim the foam from the surface and carefully drain the ghee into a glass jar, leaving the solids behind. Store in the refrigerator.

TAMARIND PASTE
Imli

Tamarind is a sour flavoring used throughout the eastern part of the world and in Mexico. The tamarind tree yields bean-like pods 5 to 8 inches in length. The outer soft shell is removed and the inner pulp and seeds are mashed into blocks for culinary use. The paste is used in marinades, chutneys, soups and refreshing sour drinks. It can be made in advance and stored in the refrigerator for at least a week. For longer periods of storage, freeze the paste.

YIELDS APPROXIMATELY 3/4 CUP

1 block tamarind (1 inch by 1 1/2 inches by 3 inches), broken into pieces
1 cup hot water

Put the tamarind pieces in a small bowl. Pour the hot water over the tamarind and keep it submerged for 30 minutes. After the tamarind has softened, loosen the fibers in the liquid, squeezing the pulp out with your fingers. Press the tamarind through a strainer into a bowl, using the back of a wooden spoon or your fingers. Discard the seeds and fibers. (Optional: For a smoother texture, push the strained mixture again through a cheesecloth.)

Stir small amounts of cold water into the paste until its consistency is a little like split pea soup. In this manner, the paste's yield can be doubled, or even tripled, before using it in a recipe.

BASMATI RICE

In north India, basmati reigns as the "queen of fragrance"—and this is no overstatement! Basmati should be served dry and fluffy with unbroken grains. Special care must be taken to rinse away the powdered residue created during the milling process. Using a shallow bowl, run cold water over the grains. With your hands, swirl the grains, then let them settle and pour off the milky water. Repeat the process until the water run-off is clear—it will require several changes of water.

DALS

No true Indian meal is complete without a dal. It is nutritious and offers an earthy taste to contrast the more complex flavors of other dishes. There are many types of dal—split peas, lentils and legumes (beans). Hulled and split legumes cook quickly and are more easily digested than other types of beans.

The following fresh flavoring ingredients are characteristic of Indian cuisine, and are included in many recipes. When getting ready for a small dinner, I usually estimate that I will need a bulb of garlic, one small ginger root, three onions, two jalapeño chilies and a single bunch of cilantro. You're guaranteed to use them.

GARLIC

Yum, garlic! This bulb grows a terrific little round, purple flower on a long stalk, but it is much better as an all-purpose flavoring agent than a garden plant. And, it has the added advantage of keeping vampires and mosquitoes away. To avoid being a bane to friends and lovers, serve them lots of garlic too.

GINGER

Fresh ginger root is prized medicinally, and is one of the great flavorings of Asian and Indian cooking. The ginger plant produces a fantastically beautiful yellow flower, which smells almost as good as the root itself. The recipes in this book call for inches of ginger. Approximate the quantity to use based on the root's average thickness—use a little more if cutting from a thin area of the root.

ONIONS

Onions serve as the base of most gravies and sauces in Indian dishes, along with garlic and ginger. The three together are referred to as the wet trinity. The yellow onion used in Indian cooking is milder and sweeter than the white onion. Refrigerate onions before cutting them to minimize eye irritation.

GREEN CHILIES

Different varieties of green chilies vary in heat rating. In general, the smaller the chili is, the hotter it is. Recipes in this book call for jalapeños. If you prefer to use another variety, adjust the quantity to your taste. Remember, the chili tip is less hot than the stem area, and removing the seeds makes the chili milder.

CILANTRO & OTHER HERBS

Fresh herbs have a flavor role that spices alone cannot perform. Cilantro, the most prevalent herb in Indian cooking, is also known as Chinese parsley and coriander greens. Many people love its flavor while to others it has a soap-like taste. If you are one of these people, substitute Italian (flat-leaf) parsley or a combination of herbs.

Indian cooking often relies on sautéing and braising for its preparations, which require many ingredients to be added in the beginning of a recipe. Don't be intimidated by the long list of items to make ready. Preparation time for each ingredient is not long, and many are thrown into the pot together. A helpful way to cook is to prepare a *mise en place*.

Mise en place is a French cooking term for preparing a tray of all the processed ingredients. Read each recipe entirely, then prepare the ingredients according to how the recipe calls for them—chop the onions, mince the garlic, etc. The items that are added together should be grouped in a dish or bowl. This format is helpful for cooking any cuisine. For Indian cuisine, give yourself a break by toasting and grinding your spices in advance. Preparing an additional and unanticipated teaspoon of cumin is a good way to burn what you have on the stove. On this point, let me say I am the voice of experience. Good luck and let's cook!

Starters, Salads, Soups
& Light Meals

PANEER AUR HERB

✤❀✤

*P*ERSIAN INFLUENCE ON NORTH INDIAN FOOD IS STRONG. THE BLENDING OF PERSIAN AND INDIAN STYLES IS GENERALLY REFERRED TO AS MUGHAL FOOD, TYPIFIED BY DISHES SUCH AS SLOW-COOKED LAMB STEW. THIS RECIPE, HOWEVER, IS DEFINITE-LY MORE PERSIAN THAN MUGHAL IN STYLE. PERSIANS HAVE A LOVE OF FRESH, FLAVORFUL HERBS AND THIS DISH MAKES A HEAPING DISPLAY OF DIFFERENTLY TEXTURED GREENERY. WHEN SERVED WITH THE HERBED RAITA (PAGE 106), IT MAKES A TERRIF-IC HORS D'OEUVRE. I HAVE NEVER FAILED TO SEE GUESTS POLISH OFF EVERY MESSY DROP!

SERVES 10

1 recipe Herbed Raita (see page 106)

A 3-inch square Bulgarian or French feta cheese

1 bunch radishes, trimmed and cut into quarters

1 bunch watercress, trimmed and left in sprigs

1 bunch green onions, trimmed and sliced into thin rounds, including the green tops

1 cup fresh mint leaves, plucked from stems

1/2 cup fresh dill, plucked from stems

3/4 cup fresh cilantro, destemmed and coarsely chopped

1/2 cup fresh basil, cut in a chiffonade (see Cooking Notes below)

1/2 bunch fresh tarragon, cut into bite-sized pieces

3/4 cup golden raisins and/or grapes, halved

3/4 cup blanched slivered almonds, toasted

1 large package soft lavosh, cut into 4-inch square pieces (see Cooking Notes below)

Prepare the herbs several hours in advance, cover to keep them fresh and refrigerate until 20 minutes before your guests arrive. Start your display by setting the feta to one side on a large platter. Approach the rest of the arrangement as if the herbs were flowers—be as creative as you wish. Juxtapose the ingredients according to texture and color for visual appeal, while maintaining the ingredients in distinct piles.

Serve the herb platter, accompanied by the cut lavosh and the raita. Allow your guests to serve themselves. Generally, the lavosh is used as a wrapper, and a piece of feta, a dollop of raita and any combination of the fresh herbs are rolled up inside. Don't forget to provide your guests with plenty of napkins!

Cooking Notes

Basil Chiffonade: The chiffonade is the easiest way to cut basil with minimal bruising of the leaves. Starting with a large leaf, stack 10-15 de-stemmed leaves in a pile. Roll the leaves carefully into a loose tube shape and slice diagonally to create 1/4-inch strips.

Finding Lavosh: Lavosh can be found in gourmet specialty shops, ethnic stores, or even supermarkets in some neighborhoods. Make sure it is very fresh before purchasing the bread. A substitute would be an unleavened flat bread like chapati (see Indian Flat Breads, page 49).

Cabbage Salad with Chili & Cumin Dressing

GOBI MIRCHI AUR JEERA

$\mathscr{T}$HIS SALAD IS A SUCCESSFUL COMBINATION OF EARTHY SPICES AND FRESH GARDEN VEGETABLES. TOASTED BROWN MUSTARD SEEDS ADD NOT ONLY TANG BUT VISUAL TEXTURE. THE CRISP, FRESH FLAVORS IN THIS RECIPE MAKE IT A PERFECT ACCOMPANIMENT TO SPICIER DISHES. FOR A LIGHT LUNCH, SERVE WITH SPICY SPLIT PEA CAKE WITH HOT TOMATO CHUTNEY (PAGE 37).

SERVES 8

8-9 cups Napa cabbage, shredded (see Cooking Notes below)

1 tablespoon vegetable oil

1 teaspoon brown mustard seeds

1/4 teaspoon cumin seeds

1 plum tomato, seeded and finely chopped (see Cooking Notes below)

1/2 anaheim chili, seeded and minced

1/4 cup fresh cilantro, chopped

For the Dressing

2 tablespoons vegetable oil

2 tablespoons onion, peeled and minced

Juice of 1 lime

1 tablespoon vinegar, preferably apple cider

1 teaspoon black pepper, freshly ground

1/2 teaspoon salt

1 teaspoon sugar

Garnish: 2 tablespoons blanched slivered almonds, toasted and coarsely chopped

Place the shredded cabbage in a large bowl. Heat the oil in a medium skillet over medium-high heat until very hot, but not smoking. Add the mustard and cumin seeds, stir once and let the mustard seeds begin to pop. Reduce heat to medium, add the tomato and chili, stir for 2 minutes. Remove from heat and allow to cool.

Combine the dressing ingredients in a small bowl and mix well. Check the dressing's flavor for balance, then pour over the cabbage. Add the tomato-chili mixture and cilantro. Toss and serve garnished with a sprinkling of almonds.

Cooking Notes

Shredding Cabbage: Core and quarter the cabbage. Cut very thin slices across the length of the cabbage.

Seeding a Tomato: Cut the tomato in half crosswise. Starting at the base of each tomato half, gently squeeze with your fingers, pushing the seeds upward and out. The motion is similar to squeezing a tube of toothpaste.

PALAK DAHI AUR IMLI

*T*HIS COMPOSED SALAD MAKES A FABULOUS PRESENTATION FOR AN ELEGANT DINNER PARTY. OR, ITS INGREDIENTS CAN BE SIMPLIFIED AND SERVED AS A LOVELY TOSSED SALAD, MAKING IT A WONDERFUL COMPANION TO ANY DINNER OR LUNCH.

SERVES 4 TO 6

1 large bunch spinach, rinsed, patted dry and stems removed

1 1/2 tablespoons lemon juice

1/4 medium red onion, peeled and sliced into very thin rings

Vinegar for soaking

2-3 small beets

1 medium carrot, peeled and shredded

2 plum tomatoes, seeded and diced

2 oranges, skin and pith removed, separated into segments (see Cooking Notes below)

2 tablespoons fresh cilantro, chopped

For the Dressing

1/2 cup lowfat yogurt

1/4 cup tamarind paste (see page 19)

2 teaspoons brown sugar

1/8 teaspoon cayenne

1/2 teaspoon coriander, toasted and ground

1/4 teaspoon cumin, toasted and ground

4 tablespoons buttermilk

1/2 teaspoon salt

If the spinach leaves are large, pile them onto a cutting board and cut a few times with a long knife into bite-sized pieces. Toss the leaves in the lemon juice and set aside. Place the onion slices in a flat, non-metallic dish and add enough vinegar to cover. Soak the onion in the vinegar for 20 minutes to mellow its intensity. Drain, rinse with cold water and drain again. Set aside.

While the onion is soaking, put the beets into a medium pan and cover with cold water. Bring to a boil, lower the heat to simmer, cover and simmer until the beets are tender, about 20 minutes. Drain the beets and run them under cold water. When cool enough to handle, trim the ends and slip or peel the skins off. Cut the beets in half and then into 1/8-inch half moon slices. Set aside.

Combine the dressing ingredients in a small bowl and mix well. Set aside.

Arrange the spinach leaves on an attractive serving platter. Scatter the onion slices and shredded carrots over the spinach and mound the tomatoes in the center. Ring the outer edge of the platter with orange segments on one side and beet slices on the other. Scatter the chopped cilantro over the top. Serve the spinach platter immediately, with the dressing on the side in a small pitcher or bowl.

Cooking Notes

Removing the Membrane of an Orange: Removing the orange segments from their slightly bitter membrane intensifies flavor and adds a brighter presentation. Remove the peel from the orange. Cut away about 1/4 inch from the top and bottom of the orange. With a small paring knife, trim the outer membrane away in panels by working the knife from top to bottom while rotating the orange. Loosen the segments from the interior membrane by running the tip of the knife between each segment and the adjacent membrane. The segments should now be loose enough to pull away. Remove any remaining seeds.

Radish Lentil Soup

*S*AMBAR, A HIGHLY FLAVORED VEGETABLE STEW, SERVES AS A
FIRST COURSE TO ALMOST ANY SOUTH INDIAN MEAL. VARIATIONS
OF SAMBAR ARE AS NUMEROUS AS SPOKEN DIALECTS IN INDIA.
THIS RECIPE CAN ALSO BE MADE WITH OKRA, EGGPLANT, POTATO
AND SPRING ONION, OR ANY COMBINATION OF VEGETABLES. FOR A
LIGHT MEAL, SERVE THE SAMBAR WITH CRUSTY PIECES OF PEAS-
ANT BREAD AND A TANGY GREEN SALAD. OR, GET NATIVE AND EAT
THE SAMBAR OVER RICE WITH YOUR FINGERS.

SERVES 6 TO 8

1 cup yellow split peas (channa dal)

1 1/2 teaspoons salt

1/4 teaspoon turmeric

2 tablespoons vegetable oil

A large pinch ground asafetida

1 1/2 teaspoons fenugreek seeds

1 1/2 teaspoons brown mustard seeds

2 medium onions, peeled and coarsely chopped

1 tablespoon sambar powder (see page 18)

1 Daikon or 2 bunches red radishes, sliced about 1/8-inch thick
(for the Daikon, cut pieces again crosswise)

6 plum tomatoes, seeded and finely chopped (see Cooking Notes, page 27)

1/2 recipe tamarind paste (see page 19)

2 teaspoons brown sugar

2 tablespoons ghee (see page 19) or vegetable oil

1/2 teaspoon fenugreek seeds

1 teaspoon brown mustard seeds
3/4 cup fresh cilantro, coarsely chopped
Salt, to taste

In a shallow dish, rinse the split peas and pick out discolored grains. Drain and place the split peas, salt, turmeric and 4 cups cold water in a large thick-sided pot. Stir to mix and bring to a boil. Reduce heat to low and simmer, partially covered, for 45 minutes. Stir occasionally toward the end and add water if the peas start to stick. Remove from heat.

In another large thick-sided pot, heat the oil over medium-high heat. Add the asafetida, fenugreek and mustard seeds. After the mustard seeds have popped, add the onions and reduce the heat to medium. Sauté the onions until they are translucent but not browned, about 5 minutes. Add the sambar powder and stir to mix. Stir in 4 cups cold water, the radishes and tomatoes. Bring the mixture to a simmer over high heat. Reduce the heat to low and simmer until the radishes are tender, about 15 minutes. Add the tamarind paste and brown sugar to the broth. Check the cooked split peas for consistency; if they have become thick and dough-like, stir in 1/2 cup water. Add the peas to the broth and stir to mix. Remove about 1/3 to 1/2 the volume to a blender, purée and return to the sambar pot.

In a small skillet, heat the ghee over medium-high heat. Add the fenugreek and mustard seeds. When the mustard seeds have popped, add the cilantro. Stir once or twice and remove from heat. Stir the herb mixture into the sambar. Salt to taste and serve.

Spinach, Sweet Corn & Cilantro Soup

PALAK BHUTTA SHORVA

*T*HIS SOUP HAS A WONDERFUL SMOKY FLAVOR IMPARTED BY THE BLACK CUMIN, CORIANDER SEEDS AND SPINACH. SWEET CORN COMBINES BEAUTIFULLY WITH THE FLAVORS HERE, MAKING THE SOUP A WARMING LIGHT SUPPER OR A FABULOUS FIRST COURSE. SERVE WITH INDIAN FLAT BREADS (PAGE 49), SAUTÉED PRAWNS IN SPICED YOGURT (PAGE 80) AND INDIAN COUSCOUS (PAGE 44).

SERVES 4 TO 6

1/2 medium onion, peeled and coarsely chopped

3 cloves garlic, peeled and coarsely chopped

A 2-inch piece fresh ginger, peeled and coarsely chopped

1-2 jalapeño chilies, seeded and coarsely chopped

Juice of 1/2 lime

2 tablespoons ghee (see page 19) or vegetable oil

4 cups fresh cilantro, coarsely chopped

1 cup fresh mint leaves, coarsely chopped

1 cup spinach leaves, washed and patted dry

1 teaspoon salt

1/2 teaspoon sugar

1 teaspoon black cumin, toasted and ground

1 teaspoon coriander, toasted and ground

1/2 teaspoon turmeric

4 ears yellow corn, parboiled and kernels cut from the cob (see Cooking Notes below)

1 teaspoon shahi masala (see page 17)

3 cups chicken or vegetable stock

1/4 cup cream

Garnish: Fresh cilantro sprigs

In a blender, combine the onion, garlic, ginger, chilies, lime juice and 2 tablespoons cold water. Purée into a fine paste and set aside.

In a Dutch oven or a skillet with 3-inch sides, heat the ghee or vegetable oil over medium-high heat. Add the onion-garlic purée and sauté for 2 minutes. Reduce the heat to medium, add the cilantro, mint, spinach, salt, sugar, black cumin, coriander and turmeric, stir and cook for 1 minute. Stir in the corn and shahi masala. Add the chicken or vegetable stock, stir again and bring to a simmer over medium-high heat. Remove about 1/2 the volume to a blender, purée and return to the Dutch oven or skillet. Stir in the cream and serve garnished with cilantro sprigs.

Cooking Notes

De-kernelling Corn: Remove the husks and silk from the corn cobs, trim the ends and cut each cob in half. Using a pot large enough to hold all the corn, fill with cold water and bring to a boil. Add the corn and boil for 5 minutes. Rinse the corn in cold water and set aside until it is cool enough to handle. Cut the kernels from the cob by standing the cut side on end, moving the knife downward and cutting the kernels away from the cob at their roots.

Semolina Crab Crêpes with Red Pepper Sauce

SOOJA DOSAI

A DOSA IS A CRÊPE-LIKE PREPARATION MADE OUT OF SPLIT GRAM BEANS (URAD DAL) AND RICE. THE CRÊPES ARE TYPICALLY SERVED FOR BREAKFAST AND HAVE AN ENJOYABLE FERMENTED FLAVOR. IN INDIA, DOSAI ARE USUALLY SERVED AS MASALA DOSAI, CRÊPES STUFFED WITH POTATO, CHILI AND SPICES. IN THIS RECIPE, THE DOSA BATTER HAS BEEN CHANGED TO ALLOW QUICKER PREPARATION. COMBINED WITH THE CRAB FILLING, THESE DOSAI MAKE A TERRIFIC STARTER COURSE OR BRUNCH ENTRÉE. ALL OF THE COMPONENTS OF THIS RECIPE CAN BE PREPARED AHEAD OF TIME; THE DOSAI, HOWEVER, SHOULD BE COOKED INTO THEIR PANCAKE FORM RIGHT BEFORE SERVING. MAKING THE PANCAKES IS A FUN JOB, AND IS PERFECT FOR A CHILD OR AN EARLY ARRIVING GUEST.

SERVES 6 ♦ 3 EACH (YIELDS 18 MINI DOSAI)

For the Dosa Batter

1/2 cup semolina flour

1 tablespoon all-purpose flour

5 tablespoons buttermilk

1 teaspoon cream

1 teaspoon vegetable oil

1/2-1 jalapeño chili, minced

3/4 teaspoon cumin, toasted and ground

1/4 teaspoon salt, or to taste

To make the dosa batter, mix together the semolina flour, all-purpose flour, buttermilk, cream and I cup cold water in a medium bowl. Let the mixture stand for 30 minutes. In a medium skillet, heat the oil over medium-high heat. Add the chili and cumin, stir and cook for 2 minutes. Stir the chili-cumin mixture and the salt into the batter. The batter should be thin, like a crêpe batter. If it is not, add cold water, I tablespoon at a time, until it thins out. Set aside until ready to cook the dosai, about 40 minutes before serving.

For the Crab Filling

3/4-1 1/2 jalapeño chilies, coarsely chopped

2 cloves garlic, peeled and coarsely chopped

A 1-inch piece fresh ginger, peeled and coarsely chopped

1/4 small onion, peeled and coarsely chopped

1 tablespoon vegetable oil

1/2 teaspoon brown mustard seeds

1/2 plum tomato, seeded and diced

1/4 medium red pepper, cored, seeded and diced

1/2 pound cooked flake crab meat

1/2 teaspoon amchoor

1/4 teaspoon garam masala (see page 17)

1/4 cup fresh cilantro, coarsely chopped

Salt, to taste

To make the crab filling, combine the chilies, garlic, ginger, onion and 2 tablespoons cold water in a blender. Purée the mixture into a fine paste and set aside. In a large skillet, heat the oil over medium-high heat. When hot, add the mustard seeds, stir and allow them to pop. Add the purée and cook until any excess water evaporates, about 3 minutes. Add the tomato and red pepper, sauté for 2 minutes. Add the crab and cook 2-3 minutes. Stir in the amchoor, garam masala and cilantro. Taste for salt, remove from heat and set aside.

For the Red Pepper Sauce

2 teaspoons vegetable oil

1 medium red pepper, cored, seeded and coarsely chopped

1/2 plum tomato, seeded and coarsely chopped

1/2 teaspoon cumin, toasted and ground

1 tablespoon cream

1/4 teaspoon salt, or to taste

To make the red pepper sauce, heat the oil in a medium skillet over medium-high heat. Add the red pepper and tomato, stir occasionally until softened, about 4 minutes. Stir and set aside to cool slightly. Transfer the red pepper-tomato mixture to a blender and add the cumin, cream and salt. Purée and set aside.

Vegetable oil for cooking dosai

Garnish: 1/2 cup fresh cilantro, finely chopped

To cook the dosai, start by placing a plate in a warm place on the range. In a large non-stick skillet, spread 1 teaspoon vegetable oil over the bottom of the skillet and heat over medium-high heat. When the oil is hot, but not smoking, pour in 1 tablespoon of dosa batter and gently rotate the skillet in a circle to distribute the batter into a thinner circle, about the size of a coaster. Cook the dosa until it is dry on top and nicely browned on the bottom, about 50 seconds. Carefully lift with tongs or a spatula and cook the other side for 50 seconds. Do not be surprised if the first two dosai stick a little. If you want to cook more dosai at once, use two skillets instead of loading up more than one dosa in a pan. Place the cooked dosa on the warm plate and cover with foil. Repeat the process using all of the batter, spreading a little more oil on the skillet if the dosai begin to stick.

To assemble the dosai, first reheat the crab filling and red pepper sauce if they have been made in advance. Keep the mixtures warm while assembling the dosai. Fill one half of each dosa with a heaping teaspoon of crab filling. Fold the dosa in half over the filling and arrange on a serving platter; they will look like little half moons. Top each dosa with a line of red pepper sauce and a sprinkle of cilantro. Serve immediately.

Spicy Split Pea Cake with Hot Tomato Chutney

❋

*F*RITTERS ARE A COMMON BREAKFAST AND SNACK FOOD IN INDIA. THEY ARE USUALLY ENJOYED WITH A CHUTNEY. THIS RECIPE EMPLOYS A GUJARATI METHOD, WHICH REMOVES MUCH OF THE OIL REQUIRED FOR DEEP-FRIED FRITTERS BY BAKING THE BATTER INTO A CAKE. THE MUSTARD AND AJWAIN SEEDS GIVE THE CAKE A SPICY TWIST YIELDING DELICIOUS RESULTS, ESPECIALLY WHEN DRAPED WITH THE THICK, EARTHY HOT TOMATO CHUTNEY (PAGE 112).

SERVES 8

1 recipe Hot Tomato Chutney (see page 112)

1/2 cup yellow split peas (channa dal)
1 ear yellow corn, husks and silk removed
1/3 pound boiling potatoes (Yukon Gold or Red Russet)
1 tablespoon ghee (see page 19) or vegetable oil
3/4 teaspoon brown mustard seeds
1/2 teaspoon cumin seeds
1/4 teaspoon ajwain seeds
3/4 jalapeño chili, minced
2 cloves garlic, peeled and minced
A 1/2-inch piece fresh ginger, peeled and chopped
1/2 cup lowfat yogurt
1/2 teaspoon baking soda
1/2 teaspoon salt
1/4 teaspoon turmeric
1/4 cup frozen peas, thawed

Rinse the split peas in a shallow bowl with several changes of cold water. Pick out the discolored grains. Keep the split peas covered with water for several hours or overnight.

In a pot, submerge the corn and potatoes in cold water and bring to a boil. Turn heat to low and simmer for 8 minutes. Remove the corn and continue to simmer the potatoes for 12 minutes. Remove the corn kernels from the cob by standing the cob on end and slicing in a downward motion at the roots of the corn kernels. Set the corn aside in a bowl. Peel the boiled potatoes and cut into 1/4-inch cubes. Add the potatoes to the corn.

Preheat the oven to 325°F. In a small skillet, heat the ghee over medium-high heat. When hot, add the mustard, cumin and ajwain seeds. After the mustard seeds pop, reduce the heat to medium, add the chili, garlic and ginger, stir the mixture briskly for about 1 minute. Remove from heat and set aside to cool slightly.

Drain the split peas in a sieve and put them into a blender. Add 1/4 cup of the yogurt, the spice mixture and 3 tablespoons cold water. Purée the mixture until it is a smooth batter. Transfer the batter to a large bowl, add the remaining yogurt, baking soda, salt and turmeric, mix well. Add the corn, potatoes and peas, mix again. Grease a 9-inch cake pan, dust it with flour and pour the batter into the pan. Smooth the batter with the back of a spoon. Place the pan on the middle rack of the oven and bake for 45 minutes, until a straw or piece of spaghetti comes out clean after poking the cake's center. Cut into wedges and serve hot with the Hot Tomato Chutney.

Grains, Legumes
& Breads

Aromatic Basmati Rice

SAADAY CHAAVAL

IN HINDI, BASMATI MEANS "QUEEN OF FRAGRANCE," AND THE NUTTY, SWEET SMELL OF BASMATI RICE IS INDEED UNMISTAKABLE. BASMATI IS A NECESSARY ELEMENT IN BIRYANI DISHES AND IS THE PREFERRED TYPE OF RICE SERVED WITH NORTH INDIAN MEALS. THE BEST GRADE OF BASMATI RICE IS FROM THE PUNJAB IN INDIA, HAS NO BROKEN GRAINS AND IS AGED AT LEAST SIX MONTHS. THE RICE IS SERVED FLUFFY, NOT STICKY. THE MILLING PROCESS CREATES RESIDUE STARCHES THAT MAKE RINSING THE GRAINS EXTREMELY IMPORTANT TO PREVENT STICKINESS.

SERVES 4 TO 6

1 1/2 cups basmati rice
Optional:
A 2-inch stick cinnamon
2 whole cloves
2 green cardamom pods, slightly crushed

In a bowl or shallow dish, wash the rice with cold water until it runs clear. Cover with water and soak for 30 minutes. Using a sieve, drain the rice thoroughly, and put into a thick-sided pot with 2 cups cold water. Add the optional spices, stir the rice mixture and bring to a boil over high heat. Immediately reduce heat to very low (between warm and low on an electric stove), cover and simmer for 25 minutes. Remove from heat and let stand for 5 minutes. Gently fluff with a fork, removing the whole spices, and serve.

Basmati Rice with Green Onion & Dill

THIS RICE DISH HAS A PLEASANT HERBAL RESONANCE AND IS EXTREMELY SUBTLE. IT IS AN EASY MATCH FOR ANY OF THE RECIPES IN THIS BOOK. TRY IT WITH RED KIDNEY BEANS IN A SPICY TOMATO BROTH (PAGE 46) AND KINGLY LAMB (PAGE 98).

SERVES 4 TO 6

1 1/2 cups basmati rice

2 tablespoons vegetable oil

1/4 teaspoon cumin seeds

1/2 cup green onion, trimmed and sliced into thin rounds, including the green tops

2 tablespoons fresh dill, plucked from stems and chopped

1/4 teaspoon garam masala (see page 17)

3/4 teaspoon salt

2 cups chicken or vegetable stock, or water

In a bowl or shallow dish, wash the rice in several changes of cold water until it runs clear. Cover with water and soak for 30 minutes. Using a sieve, drain the rice thoroughly and set aside.

Heat the oil in a thick-sided pot over medium-high heat. When very hot, add the cumin seeds and let them sizzle for 30 seconds. Add the green onion and stir for another 15 seconds. Stir in the rice, dill, garam masala and salt. Stir to mix and fry the rice mixture for 2 minutes. Stir in the chicken or vegetable stock, or water. Turn the heat up to high and bring the mixture to a boil. Immediately turn the heat to very low, cover and simmer until the rice is tender but not mushy, about 20 minutes. Gently fluff with a fork to mix the ingredients and serve.

Basmati Rice with Lima Beans & Currants

KISHMISH CHAAVAL

❋

*T*HIS RICE DISH HAS A COMFORTABLE EARTHY AROMA WITH A SLIGHTLY SWEET FLAVOR. IT'S A TERRIFIC MEAL IN ITSELF WHEN SERVED WITH A RAITA, SUCH AS GARDEN VEGETABLE RAITA WITH BROWN MUSTARD SEEDS (PAGE 107). IT IS ALSO A WONDERFUL ACCOMPANIMENT TO PRAWNS SPICED WITH FENUGREEK SEEDS AND LIME (PAGE 78) OR KINGLY CHICKEN SCENTED WITH CLOVES AND BLACK CUMIN (PAGE 88).

SERVES 4 TO 6

1 1/2 cups basmati rice

2 tablespoons vegetable oil

1/2 teaspoon brown mustard seeds

1/2 teaspoon cumin seeds

1/2 medium onion, peeled and finely chopped

4 tablespoons currants

1/4 teaspoon turmeric

3/4 teaspoon salt

1/4 teaspoon garam masala (see page 17)

1 cup frozen baby lima beans, thawed

In a bowl or shallow dish, wash the rice in several changes of cold water until it runs clear. Cover with water and soak for 30 minutes. Using a sieve, drain the rice thoroughly and set aside.

Heat the oil in a medium thick-sided pot over medium-high heat. When very hot, add the mustard and cumin seeds. Let the mustard seeds begin to pop, about 30 seconds. Add the onion, stirring occasionally until it starts to brown, about 5 minutes. Stir in the currants. When the currants begin to puff, about 2 minutes, add the turmeric, salt, garam masala, lima beans and drained rice. Stir to mix well and sauté the rice mixture for 2 minutes. Stir in 2 cups cold water, raise the heat to high and bring the mixture to a boil. Immediately turn the heat to low, cover and simmer for 20 minutes. Gently fluff with a fork to mix the ingredients and serve.

◆

*Two smiling faces in the spice hills
of Thekkady, these girls live on
a black pepper farm.*

◆

Indian Couscous

*U*PPAMA, ALSO KNOWN AS COUSCOUS, SEMOLINA OR FARINA, IS THE BREAKFAST DISH OF SOUTH INDIA. IN KEEPING WITH WESTERN MEAL PREFERENCES, IT CAN BE SERVED AS A FANTASTIC LIGHT MEAL WITH A FISH DISH LIKE PAN-FRIED TROUT WITH GINGER AND MUSTARD SEEDS (PAGE 84) AND GARDEN VEGETABLE RAITA WITH BROWN MUSTARD SEEDS (PAGE 107).

SERVES 6

2 tablespoons yellow split peas (channa dal)

2 tablespoons vegetable oil

1 teaspoon brown mustard seeds

1/2 teaspoon cumin seeds

1 teaspoon urad dal

A large pinch ground asafetida

1/2-1 jalapeño chili, minced

2 bay leaves, torn into pieces

3 tablespoons raw cashews, broken into pieces

2 cups couscous (semolina or farina)

1/2 teaspoon salt

2 cups boiling water

1/3 cup golden raisins

1/2 cup fresh cilantro, coarsely chopped

Garnish: Yogurt or raita, fresh cilantro sprigs, tomato wedges and cucumber spears

In a small saucepan, bring the split peas and 1/2 cup of cold water to a boil. Boil until the split peas are tender but still firm, about 5 minutes. Drain and set aside.

In a medium pot, heat the oil over medium-high heat. When hot, add the mustard and cumin seeds, urad dal and asafetida. After the mustard seeds pop, about 30 seconds, add the chili, bay leaves, cashews and drained split peas. Sauté the mixture until the nuts begin to brown, about 3 minutes. Add the couscous and stir to mix well. Add the salt, boiling water, raisins and cilantro. Stir to mix, remove from heat, cover and let stand for 5 minutes. Fluff with a fork and serve with garnish.

Red Kidney Beans in a Spicy Tomato Broth

RAJMA DAL

❊

*A*LL OVER INDIA, DALS – LENTILS, SPLIT PEAS AND BEANS – ARE CONSIDERED AN INTEGRAL PART OF A MEAL. IN THIS RECIPE, THE INCREDIBLE CARAMEL-SCENTED GHEE IS USED TO INFUSE AROMA AND FLAVOR INTO THE DISH. TRY IT WITH SPINACH AND MUSTARD GREENS WITH URAD DAL AND POTATOES (PAGE 64) AND, OF COURSE, A COOLING RAITA.

SERVES 8

2 cups dried red kidney beans

1 large onion, peeled and coarsely chopped

4 cloves garlic, peeled and minced

A 2-inch piece fresh ginger, peeled and minced

3 tablespoons ghee (see page 19)

1/2 teaspoon turmeric

1/2-1 teaspoon cayenne

1 teaspoon coriander, toasted and ground

2 bay leaves, torn into pieces

1 teaspoon salt

2 teaspoons vegetable oil

1 1/2 teaspoon cumin seeds

1 teaspoon brown mustard seeds

1/2 teaspoon ground asafetida

1 16-ounce can chopped tomatoes with juice

1 teaspoon garam masala (see page 17)

Garnish: 1/4 cup fresh cilantro, chopped

Soak the beans in 4 cups of water for at least 8 hours.

Drain the beans in a sieve, rinse and put into a Dutch oven or skillet with at least 3-inch sides. Add the onion, garlic, ginger, 1 1/2 tablespoons of the ghee, turmeric, cayenne, coriander, bay leaves, salt and 4 cups cold water. In a small skillet, heat the oil over medium-high heat. When hot, add the cumin, mustard seeds and asafetida. Let the spices sizzle and pop, about 30 seconds. Remove from heat and pour into the bean pot. Stir the mixture to blend the ingredients and bring to a boil over high heat. Reduce heat to low, cover and simmer 30 minutes.

Remove the lid, add the tomatoes and return to a boil. Reduce heat to low and simmer uncovered until the beans are soft, about 25-35 minutes. If necessary, add more water and cook longer to make the beans tender. Stir in the garam masala and cook for another 5 minutes. Mix in the remaining ghee and serve garnished with cilantro.

Lentils with Panch Phoran

BENGALI TIMATAR DAL

LEGUMES – LENTILS, SPLIT PEAS AND BEANS – ARE REFERRED TO IN HINDI AS "DAL." HULLED DAL COOKS QUICKLY, BECOMING A PURÉE AND A DELICIOUS SIDE DISH. MOONG DAL IS THE HULLED AND SPLIT MUNG BEAN ADORED FOR ITS FLAVOR. MASOOR DAL IS A RED LENTIL. TOGETHER WITH A LITTLE TOMATO AND PANCH PHORAN, THESE LEGUMES MAKE A FRAGRANT DISH.

SERVES 4 TO 6

1/2 cup masoor dal
1/2 cup moong dal
3/4 teaspoon salt
2 teaspoons vegetable oil
A large pinch ground asafetida
1/2 teaspoon panch phoran (see page 18)
1 plum tomato, seeded and finely chopped
1/4 teaspoon turmeric

In a bowl or shallow dish, rinse the dal well and pick out discolored grains. Drain in a sieve and put into a thick-sided pot with the salt and 3 cups cold water. Stir to mix and bring to a boil. Reduce heat to low and simmer for 25 minutes. Stir occasionally, especially near the end, to prevent sticking. (Note: If this recipe is doubled the cooking time is longer, about 45 minutes. Check to make sure the lentils are soft before removing them from the heat.)

While the dal is cooking, heat the oil in a small skillet over medium-high heat. Add the asafetida and panch phoran, stir and allow the spices to sizzle and pop, about 30 seconds. Add the tomato and turmeric. Work the mixture with a wooden spoon into a purée. After 3 minutes, add the tomato mixture to the cooked dal, simmer for 2 more minutes and serve.

CHAPATI

CHAPATI, INDIAN FLAT BREADS, ARE ONE OF THE STAPLE BREADS OF NORTH INDIA. TORN PIECES OF CHAPATI SERVE AS FORKS TO SCOOP UP MORSELS ON THE PLATE, OR THALI. ♦ TRADITIONALLY, THESE FLAT BREADS ARE COOKED IN A SKILLET, AS THEY ARE IN THIS PREPARATION, AND THEN FINISHED OVER HOT COALS. SERVE THE CHAPATI WITH RICE AND OTHER DISHES FOR A TRUE INDIAN MENU. OR, FOR A LIGHT SNACK, TRY THEM FOLDED AND STUFFED WITH SPICED GROUND BEEF WITH PEAS AND CARROTS (PAGE 96).

SERVES 4 TO 6

1 cup whole wheat flour
1 cup all-purpose flour, plus 1/4 cup set aside for dusting
1/2 teaspoon salt
3/4-1 cup warm water
3 tablespoons ghee (see page 19), warmed, for brushing chapati

Combine the flours and salt in a large bowl and mix well. Stir 3/4 cup of the warm water into the flour mixture and work into a soft dough. If the dough is too dry, add more water 1 tablespoon at a time, working in the water after each addition, until the dough is soft but not sticky. If it becomes sticky, work a little more flour into the dough.

Dust a smooth work surface with some flour and place the dough on it. Knead the dough until it is elastic and pliable, about 8 minutes. Form the dough into a ball and place in a lightly oiled bowl. Cover the bowl with a damp towel and allow to rest in a warm place for 30 minutes.

Once again, turn the dough out onto a flour-dusted surface and knead it briefly. Don't knead the dough too much or it will become tough. Divide the dough into 10-12 small balls and keep them covered with the damp towel as you work.

With a rolling pin, flatten each dough ball into a 6-inch very thin disk. While working the dough, sprinkle the surface with a little flour to prevent sticking. Work the rolling pin over its surface and continue to roll in different directions to keep the disk round.

Heat a large non-stick skillet over medium-high heat, add a chapati and cook until it begins to bubble and puff, about 1 minute. Turn and cook the other side for 30 seconds; both sides should be covered with brown flecks. Brush one side with ghee and wrap in a towel to keep warm. Repeat with the remaining chapati and serve warm.

Garden Vegetables
Roots & Squash

BADAM PAIR RAI

THIS PREPARATION OF SUCCULENT GREEN BEANS IS TYPICAL OF BENGAL. THE SELECTION OF INGREDIENTS AND THEIR CHOPPING, ROASTING AND GRINDING IS A WELL-DEFINED RITUAL IN BENGAL. VEGETABLES ARE CHOSEN FOR THEIR FRESHNESS, COLOR, TEXTURE AND SHAPE. USE THE MOST TENDER BEANS FOR THIS DISH AND TRY SERVING IT WITH INDIAN COUSCOUS (PAGE 44).

SERVES 4 TO 6

1 pound green beans, broken into 1 1/2-inch pieces
1/4 teaspoon salt
1 tablespoon vegetable oil
1/4 teaspoon kalonji seeds
1 teaspoon brown mustard seeds
1/4 medium onion, peeled and sliced
3 cloves garlic, peeled and minced
1/4 teaspoon cayenne
1/2 teaspoon turmeric
Juice of 1/2 lemon
1/4 teaspoon black pepper, freshly ground
Salt, to taste

Garnish: 3 tablespoons blanched slivered almonds, toasted and coarsely chopped

Fill a large pot with enough water to cover the beans and bring to a boil. Add the beans and 1/4 teaspoon salt, boil for 3 minutes. Drain and set aside.

In a large skillet, heat the oil over medium-high heat. Add the kalonji and mustard seeds, stir until they begin to pop, about 30 seconds. Add the onion and sauté until it begins to brown, about 3-4 minutes. Add the garlic and cook another 2 minutes. Add the cayenne and turmeric, stir a few times, add the green beans and lemon juice. Stir and cook until the beans are heated through, about 2 minutes. Stir in the black pepper and salt to taste. Serve garnished with the almonds.

♦

A mere forty-five minutes by boat from the thriving metropolis of Bombay, the ladies of Elephanta Island live a traditional life. Every morning the water jugs are used to carry the day's supply from the well.

♦

Cabbage with Panch Phoran & Carrots

GAJAR AUR BANDH GOBI

THIS DISH IS ALMOST LIKE A WARM SALAD. IT HAS AN EARTHY FLAVOR FROM THE CABBAGE, WHICH IS SPIKED BY THE BENGALI NOTES OF PANCH PHORAN AND THE SWEETNESS OF CARROTS AND RAISINS. FOR AN APPEALING COMBINATION OF FLAVORS, SERVE THIS DISH WITH GOAN SPICED DUCK (PAGE 91) AND TAMARIND GINGER CHUTNEY WITH KALONJI AND TART APPLES (PAGE 111).

SERVES 6 TO 8

1 1/2 tablespoons vegetable oil

1/2 cup raw cashews

3 tablespoons golden raisins

A large pinch ground asafetida

3/4 teaspoon panch phoran (see page 18)

1/4 medium onion, peeled and finely chopped

1/3 pound carrots, peeled, ends trimmed and julienne cut (see Cooking Notes below)

1 small cabbage (about 1 pound), cored and shredded (see Cooking Notes, page 27)

A large pinch-1/8 teaspoon cayenne

1/8 teaspoon ajwain, toasted and ground

1/4 teaspoon salt, or to taste

2 tablespoons lowfat yogurt

Freshly ground black pepper, to taste

In a small skillet, heat 1/2 tablespoon of the oil over medium-high heat. When hot, add the cashews and raisins. Stir frequently until the cashews have browned and the raisins have puffed up, about 3 minutes. Remove from heat and set aside.

Heat the remaining oil over medium-high heat in a Dutch oven or skillet with at least 3-inch sides. When hot, add the asafetida and panch phoran, let the spices sizzle for 30 seconds. Add the onion and sauté until softened, about 3 minutes. Add the carrots and sauté for 2 minutes. Add the cabbage, cayenne, ajwain, salt and 1 tablespoon of water. Stir to mix well, cover, turn heat to low and simmer for 5 minutes. Stir in the cashew mixture, yogurt and black pepper. Cook for 1 more minute and serve.

Cooking Notes

Carrots Julienne: Start by cutting the carrots, or any other vegetable, into 2-inch long segments. Work the knife along the length of each carrot segment to cut 1/8-inch slices. Stack the carrot slices on top of one another and cut along the length again, making 1/8-inch matchsticks, otherwise known as "carrots julienne."

Braised Cauliflower with Panch Phoran Yogurt Sauce

PANCH PHORAN AUR PHOOL GOBI

HIS PARTICULAR DISH IS ENHANCED BY THE BACKGROUND FLAVORS OF PANCH PHORAN: SWEET FENNEL, PUNGENT KALONJI, HOT MUSTARD, EARTHY CUMIN AND THE INDESCRIBABLE FENUGREEK. TRY THIS CAULIFLOWER DISH WITH ITS AROMATIC YOGURT SAUCE IN COMBINATION WITH SALMON WITH AJWAINI MUSTARD GREENS (PAGE 82), HERBED RAITA (PAGE 106) AND TAMARIND GINGER CHUTNEY (PAGE 110).

SERVES 6 TO 8

1 small onion, peeled and coarsely chopped

3 cloves garlic, peeled and coarsely chopped

A 1-inch piece fresh ginger, peeled and coarsely chopped

1 cup lowfat yogurt

1/2 teaspoon salt

1 teaspoon sugar

1 head cauliflower (about 2 pounds), separated into bite-sized florets

3 tablespoons vegetable oil

2 whole cloves

2 green cardamom pods

A 3/4-inch piece cinnamon

1 teaspoon panch phoran (see page 18)

Salt, to taste

1/4 cup fresh cilantro, coarsely chopped

In a blender, combine the onion, garlic, ginger and 2 tablespoons of cold water. Purée and transfer half of the paste to a large bowl with the yogurt, salt and sugar. Stir to combine. Mix in the cauliflower florets, turn the florets in the marinade to coat thoroughly and set aside.

In a large skillet, heat the oil over medium-high heat until very hot, but not smoking. Add the cloves, cardamom pods, cinnamon and panch phoran, stir and allow the spices to sizzle and pop, about 30 seconds. Add the remaining half of the garlic-ginger purée and stir for 2 more minutes. Add the cauliflower-yogurt mixture and cook for 3 minutes. Reduce the heat to low, cover and let the cauliflower simmer for 5 minutes. Uncover the pot and finish cooking until the cauliflower is tender, about 12-15 minutes. Check for salt, stir in the cilantro and transfer to a serving dish.

Creamy Roasted Eggplant with Shahi Masala

✤✤✤

*T*EXTURE, SMELL, TASTE AND VISUAL APPEARANCE ARE ALL VERY IMPORTANT IN AN INDIAN MEAL. THIS ELEGANT DISH SHOWCASES THE CREAMY TEXTURE OF THE EGGPLANT AND THE RICH AROMA OF THE SHAHI MASALA SPICE BLEND. THE MASALA INCORPORATES FRAGRANT CARDAMOM AND FENNEL, AS WELL AS THE EARTHY FLAVORS OF TURMERIC AND ASAFETIDA.

SERVES 6 TO 8

2 large eggplant (about 3 pounds)

3 tablespoons vegetable oil

1-2 jalapeño chilies, seeded and coarsely chopped

3 cloves garlic, peeled and coarsely chopped

A 1 1/2-inch piece fresh ginger, peeled and coarsely chopped

1/2 large onion, peeled and coarsely chopped

2 tablespoons lemon juice

4 plum tomatoes, seeded and diced (see Cooking Notes, page 27)

1/2 teaspoon turmeric

1 teaspoon cumin, toasted and ground

1 teaspoon salt

1 teaspoon shahi masala (see page 17)

1/4 cup cream

1/4 cup fresh cilantro, coarsely chopped

Garnish: 2 limes, cut into wedges

Preheat oven to 450°F. Cut each eggplant in half. Using 1 tablespoon of the oil, brush each cut side of the eggplant with oil. Place each eggplant piece, cut side facing downward, on an oiled baking sheet. Place the baking sheet in the oven on a single rack and roast until the eggplant is tender, about 30 minutes. Set aside to cool. While the eggplant is cooling, place the chilies, garlic, ginger, onion and lemon juice in a blender and purée into a paste. Set aside.

Scoop the flesh from the eggplant into a medium bowl and whip with a fork into a rough purée. Set aside.

In a large skillet, heat the remaining oil over medium-high heat, add the onion-garlic paste and sauté 3-4 minutes. Add a little water, if necessary to prevent sticking. Add the tomatoes, turmeric, cumin and salt, sauté for 5 minutes. Add the eggplant purée to the mixture and heat through, about 3 minutes. Stir in the shahi masala, cream and cilantro and cook for 1 minute. Remove from heat, transfer to a serving dish and serve garnished with lime wedges.

Eggplant Stuffed with Ajwaini Spinach & Couscous

BHARA BAIGAN

※※※

*T*HIS IS AN ELEGANT PREPARATION OF A VERY POPULAR VEG-ETABLE IN INDIAN COOKING, THE EGGPLANT. TINY BABY EGGPLANT ARE AVAILABLE IN INDIA, BUT DUE TO THEIR RARITY IN THE WEST, THIS RECIPE USES JAPANESE EGGPLANT. THE SPINACH STUFFING IS ENHANCED BY THE HOT TANGINESS OF AJWAIN. HOT TOMATO CHUTNEY (PAGE 112) PROVIDES THE PERFECT FINISH FOR THE EGG-PLANT. OVERALL, THE DISH HAS A HEARTY, FLAVORFUL IMPACT AND MAKES AN EXCELLENT VEGETARIAN MAIN COURSE.

SERVES 8

1 recipe Hot Tomato Chutney (see page 112)

8 Japanese eggplant, stems trimmed

2 tablespoons vegetable oil

Freshly ground black pepper, to taste

Salt, to taste

1/2 teaspoon ajwain seeds

1/2 teaspoon fenugreek seeds

2 cloves garlic, peeled and minced

A 1 1/2-inch piece fresh ginger, peeled and minced or grated

3/4 pound spinach, stems removed and coarsely chopped

1/4 teaspoon salt

1/2 teaspoon black pepper, ground

1/4 cup couscous, toasted

2 tablespoons ghee (see page 19), warmed, or olive oil

Preheat oven to 450°F. Slit each eggplant lengthwise, being careful not to cut all the way through to the back. Using 1 tablespoon of the oil, brush the interior of the eggplant and sprinkle the insides with black pepper and salt. Place the eggplant side by side in an oiled baking dish and set aside.

In a large skillet, heat the remaining oil over medium-high heat, add the ajwain and fenugreek seeds, stir once and allow the spices to sizzle for 30 seconds. Add the garlic and ginger, sauté for 2 minutes. Add the spinach and cook until wilted, about 3 minutes. Add the salt, pepper and couscous to the spinach mixture. Stir to mix and remove from the heat.

Stuff each eggplant with 2 spoonfuls of the spinach-couscous mixture. Bake the eggplant uncovered until soft, about 20 minutes. Drizzle with ghee or olive oil and return to the oven for another 5 minutes. Serve topped with the Hot Tomato Chutney.

Roasted Okra with Amchoor & Tomatoes

AMCHOOR BHINDI TIMATAR

*O*KRA, OR LADIES' FINGERS, IS A VERY POPULAR VEGETABLE IN INDIA. IT MUST BE PREPARED PROPERLY TO PREVENT ITS SLIMY NATURE FROM OVERWHELMING A DISH. THE INDIAN HOME COOK PROVIDES A COUPLE OF RULES OF THUMB FOR OKRA PREPARATION: FIRST, USE THE OKRA WHOLE AND SECONDLY, ROAST OR STIR FRY AT HIGH HEAT BEFORE ADDING OTHER INGREDIENTS. THIS RECIPE ROASTS THE OKRA BEFORE MIXING IT INTO A SAUTÉ. THE RESULT IS DELICIOUS! TRY SERVING THIS DISH WITH SPICY POTATOES WITH AMCHOOR AND DILL (PAGE 66) AND KINGLY CHICKEN SCENTED WITH CLOVES AND BLACK CUMIN (PAGE 88).

SERVES 6

1 1/2 pounds okra, stems trimmed

1 1/2 teaspoons amchoor, well crumbled

3 tablespoons vegetable oil

3/8 teaspoon fennel seeds

1 1/2 medium onions, peeled and finely chopped

A 2-inch piece fresh ginger, peeled and minced or grated

8 cloves garlic, peeled and minced

1-1 1/2 jalapeño chilies, minced

9 plum tomatoes, seeded and coarsely chopped (see Cooking Notes, page 27)

1/4 teaspoon turmeric

3/4 teaspoon coriander, toasted and ground

3/4 teaspoon cumin, toasted and ground

3/8 teaspoon shahi masala (see page 17)

1/4 teaspoon salt, or to taste

Garnish: 3 tablespoons fresh cilantro, coarsely chopped and 1 lemon, cut into 6 wedges

Preheat the broiler with the rack on the top notch. Place the okra in a rectangular roasting pan large enough to hold them in a single layer. Toss the okra with the amchoor and broil for 10 minutes, stirring once after 5 minutes. Set aside.

Heat the vegetable oil in a large skillet over medium-high heat. When hot, add the fennel seeds and let them sizzle for 30 seconds. Add the onion and stir until it starts to brown, about 5 minutes. Mix in the ginger, garlic and chili. Let the mixture brown for 3-4 minutes, being careful not to let it stick. Add the tomatoes, turmeric, coriander, cumin and shahi masala, stir until the tomatoes begin to soften and the excess juice has evaporated, about 3 minutes. Add the okra and stir gently to mix. Let the okra heat through and the mixture dry out, about 2-4 minutes. Add the salt, taste for flavor balance and serve garnished with the cilantro and lemon wedges.

♦

Everywhere in India, vendors sell their fresh vegetables and fruits. Dr. Swambinath's "Green Revolution" deserves the credit for the plentiful food supply today. He encouraged land reform in India with a pledge to create a livelihood for many families through subsistence farming.

♦

Spinach & Mustard Greens with Urad Dal & Potatoes

MUSTARD GREENS ARE COMMONLY EATEN IN THE EASTERN PART OF THE WORLD, AND THEY ADD A PIQUANT FLAVOR TO THIS RECIPE. IF YOU HAVE TROUBLE FINDING THEM, SUBSTITUTE SPINACH. SEE IF YOU CAN TASTE THE NUTTY FLAVOR ADDED BY THE URAD DAL IN THIS DISH—IT IS AN EXAMPLE OF A BEAN BEING USED AS A SPICE.

SERVES 6

1 1/2 pounds boiling potatoes (Yukon Gold or Red Russet)

4 tablespoons vegetable oil

1 teaspoon urad dal

20 fenugreek seeds

3 cloves garlic, peeled and minced

A 1 1/2-inch piece fresh ginger, peeled and minced or grated

1/4-1/2 jalapeño chili, minced

1 teaspoon amchoor, well crumbled

2 teaspoons coriander, toasted and ground

1/2 pound spinach, stems trimmed and roughly chopped

1/2 pound mustard greens, stems trimmed and roughly chopped

3/4 teaspoon shahi masala (see page 17)

1/2 teaspoon salt

Scrub the potatoes, place in a medium pot and cover with water. Bring to a boil, reduce heat to low and cover. Simmer until fork-tender, about 20-25 minutes. Drain and rinse the potatoes in several changes of cold water and let stand. When cool enough to handle, peel and cut the potatoes into 1/2-inch cubes. Place the potatoes in a bowl and toss with 2 tablespoons of the oil.

In a Dutch oven or skillet with at least 3-inch sides, heat the remaining oil over medium-high heat. When hot, add the urad dal and fenugreek seeds, sauté until the dal becomes golden, about 2-3 minutes. Add the garlic, ginger and chili, stir and cook for 2 or 3 minutes longer. Add the potatoes and sprinkle with the amchoor and coriander. Stir to mix, lower the heat to medium and brown the potatoes for about 8 minutes while stirring frequently. Add 1/3 cup cold water and stir to mix. Add the spinach and mustard greens over the potatoes—don't mix them in yet. Cover and let the greens wilt for 3 minutes. Uncover the pot, stir and cook for 3 more minutes. Stir in the shahi masala and salt, taste for salt and serve.

Spicy Potatoes with Amchoor & Dill

THE STREET VENDORS OF INDIA OFTEN SELL THEIR FRESH CUCUMBERS AND GREEN MANGOES WITH A DRY DRESSING OF CAYENNE AND SALT. A LEMON WEDGE IS DIPPED INTO THE MIXTURE AND THEN SPREAD ONTO THE SURFACE OF THE VEGETABLE OR FRUIT. IN THE STYLE OF THE STREET VENDORS, THIS RECIPE CREATES A LIP-SMACKING EFFECT WITH THE STARCHY POTATO, SOUR AMCHOOR, HOT CHILI AND SALT. THE FRESH DILL ADDS AN HERBACEOUS FLAVOR DIMENSION.

SERVES 4 TO 6

1 1/2 pounds boiling potatoes (Yukon Gold or Red Russet)

4 tablespoons vegetable oil

3/4 teaspoon cumin seeds

1/8 teaspoon turmeric

A 1/2-inch piece fresh ginger, peeled and minced or grated

1 1/4 teaspoon amchoor, well crumbled

1/2 teaspoon salt

1/4-1/2 teaspoon cayenne

2 plum tomatoes, seeded and chopped

2 teaspoons fresh dill, plucked from stems and chopped

Garnish: 10 lemon wedges

Scrub the potatoes, place in a medium pot and cover with water. Bring to a boil over high heat, reduce heat to low and cover. Simmer until fork-tender, about 20-25 minutes. Drain and rinse the potatoes in several changes of cold water and let stand. When cool enough to handle, peel and cut the potatoes into 1/2-inch cubes. Place the potatoes in a bowl and toss with 2 tablespoons of the oil.

In a heavy skillet, heat the remaining oil over medium-high heat. When hot, add the cumin seeds and turmeric. Swirl and allow the spices to sizzle for about 30 seconds. Add the potatoes and ginger. Turn the mixture from underneath with a spatula to mix well. Sprinkle the amchoor, salt and cayenne over the potatoes and mix. Add the tomatoes, mix again and lower the heat to medium. Allow the mixture to brown, about 10 minutes. With the spatula, occasionally scrape the flavorful crust from the skillet surface while turning the potatoes. Let the mixture get very dry, but don't let it burn. Mix in the dill, transfer to a small platter and serve garnished with lemon wedges.

Potatoes with Garam Masala & Spicy Tomato

GARAM MASALA AUR TIMATAR ALOO

*T*HIS RECIPE IS A GREAT BASIC DISH WITH WONDERFUL FLAVOR AND WIDE APPEAL. IT CAN BE MIXED WITH ANY NUMBER OF MORE COMPLEX DISHES, PROVIDING AN ANCHOR FOR THE PALATE. TRY IT WITH KINGLY LAMB (PAGE 98). THE GARAM MASALA IN THE SAUCE PROVIDES NICE AROMA AND A WARMING FLAVOR.

SERVES 4

1 pound boiling potatoes (Yukon Gold or Red Russet)

3 tablespoons vegetable oil

A large pinch ground asafetida

1 medium onion, peeled and coarsely chopped

2 cloves garlic, peeled and minced

A 1-inch piece fresh ginger, peeled and minced or grated

1/2 teaspoon turmeric

1 teaspoon coriander, toasted and ground

1 teaspoon cumin, toasted and ground

1/4-1/2 teaspoon cayenne

5 plum tomatoes, seeded and coarsely chopped (see Cooking Notes, page 27)

1/2 teaspoon garam masala (see page 17)

1/2 teaspoon salt

4 tablespoons cilantro, coarsely chopped

Scrub the potatoes, place in a medium pot and cover with water. Bring to a boil over high heat, reduce the heat to low and cover. Simmer until fork-tender, about 20-25 minutes. Drain and rinse the potatoes in several changes of cold water and let stand. When cool enough to handle, peel and cut the potatoes into 1/2-inch cubes. Place the potatoes in a bowl and toss with 2 tablespoons of the oil.

Heat the remaining oil over medium-high heat in a medium saucepan or skillet. When hot, add the asafetida, stir and let sizzle for 30 seconds. Add the onion and sauté until it begins to brown, about 5 minutes. Add the garlic and ginger, stir and cook for 2-3 minutes. Add the potatoes, turmeric, coriander, cumin and cayenne. Stir well to evenly coat the potatoes with the spices and add 1/3 cup cold water. Add the tomatoes, stir again, cover and cook for 10 more minutes, stirring once after 5 minutes. Mix in the garam masala, salt and cilantro. Taste for salt and serve.

Turnips Divine with Almonds & Spices

AFTER TRYING THIS DISH, YOU WILL NEVER LOOK AT A TURNIP IN THE SAME WAY AGAIN! IT'S FABULOUS WITH FRESH MINT AND PARSLEY CHUTNEY (PAGE 109) AND SPICY MEATBALLS WITH GARAM MASALA TOMATO CURRY (PAGE 102). WHEN SELECTING YOUR TURNIPS, PURCHASE THE SMALLER ONES THAT ARE NO MORE THAN 2 1/2 INCHES IN DIAMETER. THE VEGETABLES SHOULD FEEL DENSE. IF THEY ARE LIGHT IN WEIGHT, THEY WILL BE WOODY AND BLAND, SORT OF LIKE A DISAPPOINTING ORANGE.

SERVES 6

1 pound turnips (or substitute 1/2 pound turnips with 1/2 pound Yukon Gold potatoes)

5 tablespoons blanched slivered almonds, toasted

2 tablespoons ghee (see page 19) or vegetable oil

A large pinch ground asafetida

1/2 teaspoon cumin seeds

1/4 teaspoon ajwain seeds

2 dried hot red chilies

1 bay leaf, torn into 3 pieces

1 medium onion, peeled, halved and sliced into half rings

1/8 teaspoon turmeric

1/4 teaspoon coriander, toasted and ground

1/8 teaspoon shahi masala (see page 17)

A pinch of black pepper, freshly ground

1/4 teaspoon salt, or to taste

In a pot, bring enough water to cover the turnips to a boil over high heat. Add the turnips and boil, partially covered, until tender, about 10 minutes. Drain and rinse the turnips in several changes of cold water to stop the cooking. When the turnips have cooled, trim the ends and peel away the thin skin using a paring knife. The turnip skin should pull away easily, leaving some of the pretty purple color behind. Cut the turnips in half, then slice crosswise into 1/8-inch thick half moons. Set aside. Using a spice/coffee grinder, pulverize 3 tablespoons of the almonds and set aside.

In a medium skillet, heat the ghee or vegetable oil over medium-high heat. When hot, add the asafetida, cumin, ajwain, chilies and bay leaf. Swirl the spices for about 30 seconds, allowing them to sizzle and infuse their flavors into the oil. Reduce heat to medium, add the onions, mix well and sauté until they soften and begin to brown, about 5 minutes. Add the turmeric and coriander, stir to mix. Add the turnips, mix well and cook another 4 minutes. If the mixture begins to dry out, add 1-2 tablespoons of water. You may have to do this several times. Stir in the ground almonds and the shahi masala and cook for 2 more minutes. Add the black pepper, salt and the remaining almonds and serve.

Roasted Butternut Squash with Ajwain & Cashews

KADDU AJWAIN AUR KOJOO

CONTRARY TO POPULAR BELIEF, ONLY ABOUT 25 PERCENT OF THE POPULATION IN INDIA IS TOTALLY VEGETARIAN. HOWEVER, VEGETABLES DOMINATE THE DIET OF ALL INDIANS. THE VARIETY OF VEGETABLES AVAILABLE, AS WELL AS THE NUMEROUS PREPARATION METHODS, ELEVATES THEM TO AN EXCITING, SUMPTUOUS AND SATISFYING PART OF THE MEAL. ◆ THE EARTHY FLAVOR AND STARCHY NATURE OF ROASTED BUTTERNUT SQUASH MAKE IT THE PERFECT VEGETABLE TO BENEFIT FROM THE UNIQUE FLAVOR OF AJWAIN. THIS DISH CAN ALSO BE PREPARED WITH PUMPKIN, ACORN SQUASH OR ANY WINTER SQUASH.

SERVES 4 TO 6

2 pounds butternut squash, peeled, cored and cut into 1-inch cubes
(see Cooking Notes below)

4 tablespoons vegetable oil

Salt, to taste

Freshly ground black pepper, to taste

1/4 cup raw cashews, broken into pieces

1/2 teaspoon ajwain seeds, slightly crushed

1 teaspoon urad dal

1/2 teaspoon cumin, ground

1/4 teaspoon turmeric

1 small onion, peeled and finely chopped

2 cloves garlic, peeled and minced

1/2-3/4 jalapeño chili, minced
2/3 cup basil, cut in a chiffonade (see Cooking Notes, page 25)

Garnish: Sprigs of basil

Raise the oven rack to the highest position and preheat to 500°F. Place the squash pieces in a bowl and toss with 2 tablespoons of the oil, salt and black pepper. Spread the squash in a single layer in a roasting pan. Roast the squash for 25-30 minutes, turning with a spatula after 15 minutes.

Heat the remaining oil in a large skillet over medium-high heat. Add the cashews and sauté until they begin to brown, about 3-4 minutes. Transfer with a slotted spoon to a plate and reserve. Add the ajwain, urad dal, cumin and turmeric to the skillet, stir to mix and cook until the spices sizzle softly. Add the onion and cook until translucent, about 4 minutes. If the mixture is sticking, add 1 or 2 tablespoons of water. Add the garlic and chili, stir and cook 2 more minutes. Add 1/4 cup cold water, the roasted squash and fried cashews. Stir gently to combine all of the ingredients. Turn the heat to low and allow the onion and nut mixture to cling to the squash, about 1 minute. Gently stir in the basil and cook for 1 more minute. Serve garnished with sprigs of basil.

Easy Squash Peeling Method: This technique will save you time and frustration in trying to get your paring knife through a tough skin on a convoluted surface. To peel the butternut squash (or any thick-skinned, rounded vegetable or fruit), start by cutting off the top and the bottom to create two flat surfaces. For pear-shaped vegetables like the butternut squash, cut into two pieces at the area that transitions from the thin neck to the wide belly. With a paring knife, remove the peel in vertical strips from top to bottom, working the knife around the circumference of the squash after each strip. Repeat the process with the second piece.

In Udaipur, city buildings are beautified with
wall paintings that have been created for religious occasions
and special family events, like weddings.
This painting is of a Rajput, coolly sniffing a flower as his
horse charges ahead. The horse is the symbol of power.
The elephant is the symbol of wealth. And, best of all, the
camel is the symbol of love. In the Indian version
of Romeo and Juliet, the amorous couple
escape on a camel.

Fish & Poultry

GARAM MASALA AUR MACHALI

*G*ARAM MASALA IS THE AROMATIC SPICE MIXTURE THAT PERMEATES THE MARINADE FOR THIS RECIPE. A TYPICAL BLEND USED IN THE MUGHAL-STYLE FOOD OF NORTH INDIA, THE MASALA ORIGINALLY MADE ITS DEBUT IN THE PUNJAB REGION. GARAM MASALA IS MUCH APPRECIATED FOR ITS AROMATIC QUALITIES, AND FOR THIS REASON IT IS GENERALLY ADDED TO A DISH IN THE LAST FIVE MINUTES OF COOKING. IN CONTRAST, THIS RECIPE USES THE BLEND'S INTRINSIC ELEMENTS FOR FLAVOR BEFORE COOKING BEGINS. IT IS A WONDERFUL COMPLEMENT TO THE MILD AND SWEET FLAVOR OF HALIBUT.

SERVES 4

1 recipe Fresh Mint and Parsley Chutney (see page 109)

1/4 small onion, peeled and coarsely chopped

A 1 1/2-inch piece fresh ginger, peeled and coarsely chopped

3 cloves garlic, peeled and coarsely chopped

1 teaspoon turmeric

1/4-1/2 teaspoon cayenne

1 teaspoon salt

1 teaspoon amchoor, well crumbled

1/2 teaspoon garam masala (see page 17)

2 tablespoons lemon juice

1 1/2 pounds halibut, cut into 4 fillets

In a blender, combine the onion, ginger, garlic, turmeric, cayenne, salt, amchoor, garam masala and lemon juice. Purée into a paste. Spread the purée over the fish fillets and marinate 1-3 hours.

Preheat the broiler with the oven rack adjusted to the second highest notch. Broil the fillets for 7-10 minutes on each side, or until the fish is firm to the touch and barely opaque (see Cooking Notes below). Brush the fillets with a little oil from the pan (or olive oil) to make the surface glisten, and serve with a dollop of Mint Chutney. For a different set of flavors, this fish can be served with Tamarind Ginger Chutney (page 110).

Cooking Fish: The rule of thumb for cooking moist fish is to use very high heat, whether frying, baking or broiling. The cooking time is 10 minutes per inch of flesh thickness. For example, if the fillet is 1 1/2-inches thick, cook each side of the fillet for 7-8 minutes. If the fillet has skin, start with the skin side up.

Prawns Spiced with Fenugreek Seeds & Lime

SPICES TRADITIONALLY USED IN PICKLING ARE THE INSPIRATION FOR THIS DISH. THE BROWN MUSTARD SEEDS AND FENUGREEK, WHEN TOASTED, IMPART THEIR UNIQUE FLAVORS TO THE MARINADE FOR THE PRAWNS. THIS DISH MAKES A PERFECT APPETIZER, OR A WONDERFUL LIGHT MEAL WHEN SERVED WITH CABBAGE SALAD WITH CHILI AND CUMIN DRESSING (PAGE 26) AND CHAPATI, OR INDIAN FLAT BREADS (PAGE 49).

SERVES 4 TO 6

2 cloves garlic, peeled and coarsely chopped
A 1 1/2-inch piece fresh ginger, peeled and coarsely chopped
1/2 teaspoon turmeric
1/2 teaspoon salt
1 1/2 teaspoons brown mustard seeds, ground
3 dried hot red chilies, toasted
1 teaspoon fenugreek seeds, toasted
Juice of 1 lime
1/4 cup vinegar
3 tablespoons vegetable oil
1 pound medium prawns (36-40 count), shelled (leave tails attached) and deveined
12 bamboo skewers, soaked in water

Garnish: Fresh cilantro, chopped

In a blender, combine the garlic, ginger, turmeric, salt, mustard seeds, chilies, fenugreek, lime juice, vinegar and oil. Purée the mixture. In a medium bowl, combine the purée with the prawns. Stir to coat evenly and allow the prawns to marinate for 30 minutes. Thread the prawns on the skewers and reserve the marinade. Grill or broil the skewers for 2-3 minutes per side, brushing the prawns with the marinade after turning them. The prawns are cooked through when they turn pink and curl. Do not overcook.

While the prawns are cooking, heat the remaining marinade in a small saucepan over medium-high heat and reduce to a thickened sauce, about 5-10 minutes. Serve the prawn skewers garnished with the cilantro. Serve the sauce in a small pitcher, or pour over the prawns on the serving dish.

Sautéed Prawns in Spiced Yogurt

BHUNA JINGA

THE DELICATELY PERFUMED MARINADE FOR THESE PRAWNS ACHIEVES ITS DISTINCT FLAVOR FROM AJWAIN, TINY SEEDS THAT RELEASE AN INCREDIBLE AROMA AND FLAVOR WHICH MELLOWS WITH COOKING. YOU WILL WANT TO SERVE THESE PRAWNS WITH RICE TO SOAK UP EVERY LAST DROP OF THE MARINADE.

SERVES 6

A 2 1/2-inch piece fresh ginger, peeled and minced or grated

2 cloves garlic, peeled and minced

Juice of 1/2 lemon

4 tablespoons lowfat yogurt

1/2 cup cream

1/4 teaspoon turmeric

1 teaspoon ajwain, toasted and ground

1 teaspoon garam masala (see page 17)

2 tablespoons vegetable oil

1 1/2 pounds medium prawns, peeled and deveined

Garnish: Fresh cilantro sprigs

In a large bowl, combine the ginger, garlic, lemon juice, yogurt, cream, spices and oil. Mix well, add the prawns and toss to coat with the marinade. Set aside and let marinate for 30 minutes. Remove the prawns from the bowl and set aside.

Transfer the marinade to a large skillet and heat over medium-high. Cook the marinade until it has thickened into a sauce, about 5 minutes. Add the prawns and mix. Turn the mixture constantly until the prawns turn opaque, pink and are curled, about 5-6 minutes. Transfer the prawns to a serving dish, leaving the excess sauce behind. Continue to cook over medium-high heat until the sauce has thickened once again. Remove from the heat and pour the sauce over the prawns. Garnish with cilantro sprigs and serve.

◆

Susan is one of the many Syrian Christians who live in the southern state of Kerala. She is holding an "idli" maker and an apparatus for scraping fresh coconut meat out of the shell. As essential as this equipment is in the households of the south, it is unheard of in the north.

◆

Salmon with Ajwaini Mustard Greens

$\mathcal{S}$ALMON IS A SLIGHTLY OILY FISH WITH FLAVORS THAT COMBINE PERFECTLY WITH THE THYME-LIKE HOTNESS OF AJWAIN AND THE SPICY TASTE OF MUSTARD GREENS. THIS DISH NOT ONLY HAS A GREAT PERSONALITY, IT IS BEAUTIFUL TO BEHOLD. TRY IT WITH SPICY POTATOES WITH AMCHOOR AND DILL (PAGE 66), CREAMY ROASTED EGGPLANT WITH SHAHI MASALA (PAGE 58) AND GARDEN VEGETABLE RAITA WITH BROWN MUSTARD SEEDS (PAGE 107).

SERVES 4

1 medium onion, peeled and coarsely chopped

2 cloves garlic, peeled and coarsely chopped

1/2-1 jalapeño chili, seeded and coarsely chopped

A 2-inch piece fresh ginger, peeled and coarsely chopped

4 tablespoons vegetable oil

1 teaspoon cumin seeds

1/4-1/2 teaspoon cayenne

1/2 teaspoon turmeric

1/4 teaspoon ajwain seeds

1/2 teaspoon salt

2 teaspoons tamarind paste (see page 19)

4 salmon steaks (7 ounces each), about 1 inch thick

2 cups mustard greens, roughly chopped

In a blender, purée the onion, garlic, chili, ginger and 2 tablespoons cold water. In a skillet large enough to hold all 4 steaks in a single layer, heat the oil over medium-high heat. When hot, add the cumin seeds and let sizzle for 30 seconds. Add the onion purée and sauté for 1 or 2 minutes. Add the cayenne, turmeric, ajwain and salt, stir and cook for 1 more minute. Stir in the tamarind paste. Add the salmon steaks and cook for 5 minutes. Turn the steaks over, sprinkle the mustard greens on top and cook for another 2-3 minutes. Quickly turn the steaks to evenly distribute the spicy mustard greens to both sides. Transfer the steaks and their greens to plates and serve.

Pan-Fried Trout with Ginger & Mustard Seeds

KHATA TALA TROUT

❈

*T*ROUT HAS A WONDERFUL FLAVOR AND IS READILY AVAILABLE IN THE UNITED STATES. THIS RECIPE UTILIZES SOME OF THE FLAVORS EXPERIENCED IN THE SOUTH INDIAN STATES OF KARNATAKA AND KERALA. THE FISH OF CHOICE IN INDIA FOR THIS RECIPE WOULD BE THE POMFRET.

SERVES 6

12-15 dried hot red chilies

3/8 teaspoon fenugreek seeds

3/4 teaspoon brown mustard seeds

12 cloves garlic, peeled and minced

A 1 1/2-inch piece fresh ginger, peeled and minced or grated

1/2 teaspoon salt

6 tablespoons lime juice

1 teaspoon tamarind paste (see page 19)

3 butterfly-cut trout (about 10 ounces each), fillets attached and heads removed

6 tablespoons ghee (see page 19)

Garnish: 6 slices lime, cut into thin half moons

Heat a small skillet over medium-high heat. Add the the chilies and fenugreek seeds and toast until fragrant and the chilies begin to darken. Transfer the spices to a spice/coffee grinder. Add the mustard seeds and pulse into a fine powder. Transfer the spices to a small bowl and add the garlic, ginger, salt, lime juice and tamarind paste. Mix well.

Rinse the trout fillets and pat dry. Open the fish and rub 1/3 of the chili paste onto the flesh of each fish. Close the fish and let marinate for 20 minutes. Heat 2 tablespoon of ghee in each of 2 large non-stick skillets over medium-high heat. (Note: the skillets must be large enough to hold the entire open fish to cook it evenly.) When the ghee is very hot, open the fish fillets, place them skin side up in the skillet and pan-fry for 1 minute. Turn quickly with a large spatula and cook for 3-4 more minutes. Remove the fish from the skillets and cover with foil to keep warm. Add the last 2 tablespoons of ghee and pan-fry the third fillet. Cut each fillet in half, garnish with lime and serve.

MASALAE WALA MURGHA

THE WORD "CURRY" WAS ORIGINALLY DEFINED NOT AS A SPICE POWDER, BUT AS A MEAT OR FISH IN A GRAVY. THE DEFINITION HAS SINCE BEEN EXPANDED TO INCLUDE VEGETABLES AS WELL. IT IS THE GRAVY THAT MAKES THIS DISH SO SUCCULENT YOU WILL WANT TO SPOON EVERY DROP FROM THE SERVING BOWL. SERVE WITH EGGPLANT STUFFED WITH AJWAINI SPINACH AND COUSCOUS (PAGE 60) AND AROMATIC BASMATI RICE (PAGE 40).

SERVES 4

2 tablespoons vegetable oil

1 medium onion, peeled and coarsely chopped

2 cloves garlic, peeled and minced

A 1-inch piece fresh ginger, peeled and minced or grated

1 teaspoon coriander, toasted and ground

3/4 teaspoon cumin, toasted and ground

1/4-1/2 teaspoon cayenne

1/2 teaspoon salt

1/4 teaspoon turmeric

1 bay leaf, torn into pieces

4 chicken breasts, skin removed (see Cooking Notes below)

7 plum tomatoes, seeded and coarsely chopped (see Cooking Notes, page 27)

1 teaspoon garam masala (see page 17)

Garnish: 3 tablespoons fresh cilantro, chopped and 1 lemon, cut into 4 wedges

Heat the oil in a large skillet over medium-high heat. When hot, add the onion and sauté ⁀ ʳ begins to brown, about 5 minutes. Add the garlic and ginger, s⁀ s. Stir in the coriander, cumin, cayenne, salt, turmeric ar⁀ ⁀ for 30 seconds. Add the chicken and turn to coat with⁀ mixture. Brown the chicken for 5 minutes, adding 1-2 table⁀ the spice mixture begins to stick to the pan.

Stir in t⁀ /2 cup water and bring to a simmer. Reduce the heat to⁀ simmer until the chicken is tender and cooked through⁀ tes. Stir occasionally to keep the chicken coated in the tom⁀ he sauce becomes dry, add 2 tablespoons of water. If inste⁀ ixture becomes soupy, remove the chicken after its cookin⁀ increase the heat to medium-high and reduce the sauce ⁀ Return the heat to low and add the chicken breasts. Stir in⁀ and cook for another 5 minutes. Serve garnished with ⁀

Cooking Notes

Removing Chicken Skin: Using a paper towel, grab the skin where it is loosest and pull the skin down and away from the meat.

Kingly Chicken Scented with Cloves & Black Cumin

A PERSIAN INFLUENCE WAS BROUGHT TO NORTH INDIAN FOOD BY THE MUGHAL COURT CIRCA 1500 AD. BLACK CUMIN, YOGURT, ALMONDS AND A SUBTLE COMBINATION OF SPICES ARE HALLMARKS OF THIS ANCIENT COOKING STYLE. THIS RECIPE, DESCRIBED BY THE WIFE OF AN INDIAN VICE ADMIRAL, WAS SERVED BY HER TO INDIA'S MODERN DAY ROYALTY, THE CABINET MEMBERS.

SERVES 4

20 whole almonds, coarsely chopped

5 whole cloves

4 green cardamom pods, slightly crushed

A 2 1/2-inch stick cinnamon

1 teaspoon coriander seeds, toasted

1 teaspoon black cumin seeds, toasted

1/4 teaspoon nutmeg, grated

1 teaspoon black peppercorns

1 dried hot red chili

1 1/2 cups lowfat yogurt

6 chicken legs, thighs and drumsticks attached, or 4 chicken breasts, skin removed (see Cooking Notes, page 87)

2 tablespoons vegetable oil

Salt to taste

Garnish: Fresh cilantro and almonds, coarsely chopped

Combine the almonds, all the spices and the chili in a spice/coffee grinder and pulverize into a fine powder. In a bowl large enough to hold all the chicken pieces, combine the spice powder with the yogurt. Score the chicken pieces in three places and add them to the yogurt. Turn to coat and marinate the chicken for at least 2 hours.

Select a thick-sided pan large enough to comfortably hold the chicken pieces without crowding. Add the oil and heat over medium-high heat. When hot, add the chicken and cook, turning the pieces with a pair of tongs, for 5 minutes. If the mixture is extremely watery, transfer the chicken to a plate and continue to cook the marinade until it is less runny, but not as thick as cake batter. Put the chicken back into the pan. Turn the heat to low, cover and simmer until the chicken is cooked through, about 20 minutes. Occasionally turn the chicken in the yogurt sauce while it is cooking, and add water if the sauce becomes too dry or sticky. When finished, the Kingly Chicken will be light brown with just enough yogurt sauce to spoon over rice. Salt to taste, garnish and serve.

BHUNA MURGHA

✾✾✾

*W*ITH BEAUTIFUL PRESENTATION AND GREAT FLAVOR, THIS DISH IS CERTAIN TO IMPRESS FRIENDS AT A PICNIC. TANDOORI USUALLY REFERS TO THE THICK-SIDED, EXTREMELY HOT OVEN USED IN INDIA. IN THIS RECIPE, SOME OF THE TRADITIONAL SPICES AND YOGURT MARINADE ARE COMBINED TO CREATE A BROILED CHICK-EN TREAT OR A BARBECUE ESPECIAL!

SERVES 4

1 teaspoon coriander, toasted and ground

1/2 teaspoon cumin, toasted and ground

1 teaspoon turmeric

1/4 teaspoon ground asafetida

1 teaspoon black pepper, freshly ground

1 teaspoon cayenne

1 teaspoon garam masala (see page 17)

1 teaspoon salt

3 cloves garlic, peeled and minced

A 1-inch piece fresh ginger, peeled and minced or grated

6 tablespoons lowfat yogurt

4 chicken breasts, skin removed (see Cooking Notes, page 87)

In a large bowl, combine all of the ingredients except the chicken. Score the chicken breasts in three places and add them to the bowl. Rub the marinade to coat the chicken and marinate for 2 hours. Preheat the grill or broiler to high heat. Place the chicken with the flesh side facing the heat and cook for 10 minutes. Turn and cook for 5 more minutes. Check to see that the chicken is cooked through by cutting the meat with a knife. If the meat is still pink, cook another 3-5 minutes. Remove the chicken from the grill or oven, baste with a little oil to make the chicken glisten and serve.

Goan Spiced Duck

❁

*T*HE SPICES AND MARINADE IN THIS RECIPE COMPLEMENT THE DELICIOUS, RICH FLAVOR OF THE DUCK AND GIVE IT A SPECTACULAR PRESENTATION. DUCK IS PRECIOUS, SO THIS RECIPE IS DESIGNED TO PROVIDE JUST A TASTE FOR EACH PERSON. IF YOU WANT TO SERVE LARGER PORTIONS OF THE MEAT, ADD ANOTHER DUCK BREAST TO THE RECIPE AND MAKE THE APPROPRIATE ADJUSTMENTS. TRY SERVING THESE DISHES AS ACCOMPANIMENTS: LENTILS WITH PANCH PHORAN (PAGE 48), BASMATI RICE WITH GREEN ONION AND DILL (PAGE 41) AND TAMARIND GINGER CHUTNEY WITH KALONJI AND TART APPLES (PAGE 111).

SERVES 4 TO 6

1 recipe Tamarind Ginger Chutney with Kalonji and Tart Apples (see page 111)

For the Goan Spice Rub
1 1/2-2 teaspoons cayenne
1 teaspoon turmeric
2 teaspoons shahi masala (see page 17)
2 teaspoons coriander, toasted and ground
2 teaspoons cumin, toasted and ground
1/2 cup lemon juice
1/2 teaspoon salt

2 Muskovy duck breasts (about 12 ounces each)

Garnish: Fresh cilantro sprigs

In a small bowl, mix together all the spices, lemon juice and salt for the rub.

With a sharp knife, score the fatty side of the duck breasts in a criss-cross manner, with scores 3/4 inch apart. Turn the duck breasts over and prick the non-fatty side with a fork. Rub the Goan spices all over the duck pieces and into the criss-cross channels. Set aside and marinate for 2 hours.

Place the oven rack in the middle position and preheat to 500°F. Line a roasting pan with foil and place the duck breasts in the pan, with the fat side facing upward. Cook until the fat has browned and the juices have just begun to run clear, about 20-25 minutes. Remove from the oven and let rest for 5 minutes. Cut the breasts into thin slices and serve neatly arranged on a platter garnished with sprigs of cilantro. Serve with the chutney on the side.

Suraj Turkey Kebabs

❦

*T*HESE DELICIOUS TURKEY PATTIES ARE NAMED FOR MY FRIEND SURAJ, WHO TAUGHT ME HOW TO EAT LIKE A GOOD HINDU . . . WITH MY HANDS! THIS DISH CAN BE SERVED AS LITTLE PATTIES OR BAKED AS A LOAF. THE LOAF HAS THE ADVANTAGE OF MAKING ATTRACTIVE LEFTOVERS FOR COLD SANDWICHES. HOT TOMATO CHUTNEY (PAGE 112) OR BENGALI MANGO CHUTNEY (PAGE 108) MAKE EXCELLENT ACCOMPANIMENTS.

SERVES 4 TO 6

1 1/4 pounds lean ground turkey

1 teaspoon urad dal

1 teaspoon coriander seeds

1/2 teaspoon cumin seeds

1/2 teaspoon fennel seeds

1/4-1/2 jalapeño chili, minced

2 cloves garlic, peeled and minced

1/2 teaspoon shahi masala (see page 17)

1/2 teaspoon black pepper, freshly ground

1/2 teaspoon salt

*5 tablespoons fresh basil leaves, cut in a chiffonade
(see Cooking Notes, page 25) and then again crosswise*

1 egg, slightly beaten

2 teaspoons flour

2 tablespoons vegetable oil

Garnish: Fresh basil sprigs

If making the turkey loaf, preheat the oven to 350°F.

Place the turkey in a large bowl. Heat a small skillet over medium-high heat. When hot, add the urad dal and toast until golden brown, 2-3 minutes. Transfer to the turkey bowl. In the same skillet, toast the coriander, cumin and fennel seeds until they release their aroma. Be careful not to burn! Transfer the spices to the turkey bowl. Add the remaining ingredients, except the oil and garnish, and mix well using your hands to evenly disperse the flavors into the meat.

If making patties, form the turkey mixture into 3-inch rounds. Heat I tablespoon of the oil in a large skillet over medium-high heat. Meanwhile, put a paper towel on a plate. When the skillet is hot, add as many patties as will fit and cook for 2-3 minutes on each side. (Alternatively, the patties can be broiled, with the oven rack adjusted to the highest notch, for 2-3 minutes on each side.) Check to make sure the centers are done. Remove the patties to the paper towel-lined plate. Dab any grease from their tops and transfer to a serving dish. Garnish with sprigs of basil and serve hot.

If making the turkey loaf, form the meat into two 3-inch by 5-inch loaves and place them into a baking dish. Bake for 45 minutes. Cut the loaves into slices and transfer them to a serving dish. Garnish with sprigs of basil.

Spiced Ground Beef with Peas & Carrots

KEEMA MATTAR AUR GAJAR KE SANGH

CUMIN PLAYS AN IMPORTANT ROLE IN INDIAN COOKING. IT IS OFTEN USED IN TANDEM WITH ANOTHER COMMON SPICE, CORIANDER. TOASTING AND GRINDING THE WHOLE SEEDS IMMEDIATELY BEFORE COOKING TEMPERS THEIR FLAVORS AND RELEASES THEIR AROMA. THIS SPICED BEEF MIXTURE CAN BE ONE IN A SERIES OF DISHES PREPARED FOR A MEAL, OR IT CAN BE FOLDED INTO INDIAN FLAT BREADS (PAGE 49), ALSO KNOWN AS CHAPATI, AND EATEN AS A SNACK.

SERVES 4 TO 6

1 medium carrot, peeled and diced

2 tablespoons vegetable oil

1 large onion, peeled and diced

2 cloves garlic, peeled and minced

A 1 1/2-inch piece fresh ginger, peeled and minced or grated

1 teaspoon cumin, toasted and ground

1 teaspoon coriander, toasted and ground

1 teaspoon cayenne

1 teaspoon turmeric

1 teaspoon salt

1 pound lean ground beef

4 plum tomatoes, seeded and chopped (see Cooking Notes, page 27)

1/2 cup frozen baby peas, thawed

1 teaspoon garam masala (see page 17)

1/4 cup fresh cilantro, chopped

Place the diced carrots in a small saucepan, cover with water and bring to a boil over high heat. Reduce the heat to low and simmer 2 minutes. Drain and set aside.

Heat the oil in a large skillet over medium-high heat. When hot, add the onion and sauté until it begins to brown, about 5 minutes. Add the garlic and ginger, sauté 2 minutes. Stir in the cumin, coriander, cayenne, turmeric and salt, cook 30 seconds. Add the ground beef, stirring to incorporate the onion-spice mixture, and brown, about 5 minutes. Add the tomatoes and 1/2 cup cold water and cook 5 minutes. Add the carrots and peas, cover and cook another 5 minutes. Stir in the garam masala and cilantro, transfer to a bowl or platter and serve.

Kingly Lamb

SHAHI KORMA

⁂

*T*HERE IS NO END TO THE IMAGINATIVE VARIETY OF INDIAN DISHES. THIS RECIPE IS AN ADAPTATION OF SHAHI MURGH–KINGLY CHICKEN SCENTED WITH CLOVES AND BLACK CUMIN (PAGE 88). THE SPICE BLEND IS VERY SIMILAR, BUT THE FLAVOR IS ELEVATED TO ANOTHER REALM WITH THE ADDITION OF TURMERIC, TOMA-TOES, GINGER, GARLIC AND ONION. TURMERIC IS A DRIED ROOT THAT HAS BEEN GROUND INTO A POWDER, AND IS BEST KNOWN FOR THE DISTINCTIVE YELLOW COLOR THAT IT IMPARTS TO A DISH. DO NOT BE INTIMIDATED BY THE LONG LIST OF INGREDI-ENTS—THE ACTUAL PREPARATION TIME IS SMALL IN EXCHANGE FOR THE INCREDIBLE TASTE OF THE TENDER LAMB AND ITS SAUCE.

SERVES 6 TO 8

For the Marinade

20 whole almonds, coarsely chopped

1 dried hot red chili

1 teaspoon black cumin seeds, toasted

1/2 teaspoon coriander seeds, toasted

5 whole cloves

3 green cardamom pods

A 3-inch stick cinnamon

1/4 teaspoon nutmeg, ground

1 teaspoon black peppercorns

2 cups lowfat yogurt

1 teaspoon salt

2 pounds boneless lamb shoulder, cut into 1 1/2-inch cubes

A 3-inch piece fresh ginger, peeled and coarsely chopped

1 whole head garlic, cloves peeled and coarsely chopped

1 large onion, peeled and coarsely chopped

1-2 tablespoons lemon juice

2 tablespoons vegetable oil

4-5 plum tomatoes, seeded and minced (see Cooking Notes, page 27)

1/4 teaspoon turmeric

Garnish: Fresh cilantro sprigs

To prepare the marinade, put the almonds, chili and all of the spices into a spice/coffee grinder and process into a fine powder. In a non-metallic bowl large enough to hold the lamb, combine the ground spices with the yogurt and the salt. Mix well, add the lamb and stir to coat. Marinate for 2 hours.

In a blender, purée the ginger, garlic, onion and lemon juice and set aside. Heat the oil in a large skillet over medium-high heat. When hot, add the ginger-garlic purée and sauté for 3 minutes. Add the tomatoes and turmeric and cook for 5 more minutes. Add the lamb and its marinade to the skillet. Turn the lamb to evenly cook all the pieces until the sauce begins to bubble, about 5 minutes. Reduce heat to simmer, cover and simmer for 1 hour, stirring occasionally. After 30 minutes, add 1/2 cup water; add more water, if necessary to prevent sticking, during the remainder of the cooking time. After an hour, the sauce should be very thick and clinging to the lamb pieces. Remove to a dish and serve garnished with sprigs of cilantro.

Lamb Scented with Cinnamon, Cilantro & Mint

KUSHU WALA GOSHT

*C*INNAMON AND MACE ARE SPICES OFTEN USED IN SWEETS, BUT THEY ARE ALSO GREAT ADDITIONS TO MANY TYPES OF MEAT. THIS DISH MAKES AN ELEGANT PRESENTATION WITH THE LOIN CHOPS. OR, YOU CAN MAKE A COMFORTING STEW-LIKE DISH BY USING LAMB SHOULDER CUT INTO PIECES. SERVE ACCOMPANIED BY A DAL, CHUTNEY, RAITA AND, OF COURSE, BASMATI RICE.

SERVES 4 TO 8

8 small lamb loin chops, or 2 1/2 pounds lamb shoulder cut into 1 1/2-inch cubes

1-2 tablespoons vegetable oil

A 1/2-inch piece cinnamon, ground

A curl of mace, ground

3/4 teaspoon cumin, ground

1 small or 1/2 large onion, peeled and coarsely chopped

3 cloves garlic, peeled and coarsely chopped

A 1-inch piece fresh ginger, peeled and coarsely chopped

1/2-1 jalapeño chili, coarsely chopped

1/2 teaspoon turmeric

1/2 teaspoon salt

2 tablespoons lemon juice

2 cups fresh cilantro, coarsely chopped

1 cup fresh mint leaves, coarsely chopped

Garnish: Sprigs of cilantro and mint leaves

Trim the lamb of excess fat; if using the chops, leave a thin layer of fat around the outside edge. In a Dutch oven or a skillet with at least 3-inch sides, heat the oil over medium-high heat. Add the cinnamon, mace and cumin. Swirl the spices until they sizzle, about 30 seconds. Add the chops and cook until brown, about 3-4 minutes on each side. If using lamb pieces, brown them while turning occasionally for 8-10 minutes. Remove the lamb to a plate. If there is a lot of oil left in the skillet, pour off all but 2 table-spoons, keeping the brownings from the meat in the skillet.

In a blender, purée the onion, garlic, ginger, chili, turmeric, salt and lemon juice. Heat the skillet again over medium-high heat and sauté the purée for 3-4 minutes. Use a wooden spoon or spatula to scrape the brownings off the bottom of the skillet as you sauté. If the mixture threatens to stick, add a tablespoon of water.

Return the browned lamb to the skillet and turn the chops or pieces in the purée. Sprinkle the cilantro and mint leaves evenly over the top of the lamb and add 1 cup water. Reduce the heat to low, cover and simmer until most of the water has evaporated and the lamb is tender, about 30 minutes. Turn the lamb occasionally, keeping it coated with the cilantro-mint mixture. Serve garnished with a small bouquet of cilantro and mint.

Spicy Meatballs with Garam Masala Tomato Curry

KOFTA KARI

*O*FTEN REFERRED TO AS "KOFTAS" IN INDIA, THESE SPICY LITTLE MEATBALLS INCORPORATE A MÉLANGE OF SPICES THAT DANCE HARMONIOUSLY ACROSS THE TONGUE. THE MELLOW NATURE OF THE FLAVORS IS ENHANCED BY TOASTING THE SEEDS, WHICH TEMPERS THE RAW SPICE. WITHOUT THIS INITIAL STEP IN PREPARATION, THE SPICES WOULD RETAIN A GREEN AND SLIGHTLY BITTER TASTE. THE REPUTATION SPICES HAVE EARNED AS BEING HARD TO DIGEST IS LARGELY DUE TO THE FACT THAT THEY ARE OFTEN IMPROPERLY USED RAW. THESE KOFTAS ARE WONDERFUL SERVED WITH AROMATIC BASMATI RICE (PAGE 40) AND CREAMY ROASTED EGGPLANT WITH SHAHI MASALA (PAGE 58).

SERVES 4 TO 6

For the Meatballs

1 pound ground lean pork

1 teaspoon urad dal

1 teaspoon coriander seeds

1/2 teaspoon cumin seeds

1/2 teaspoon fennel seeds

1/2 jalapeño chili, seeded and minced

1/4 medium onion, peeled and minced

1/2 teaspoon garam masala (see page 17)

1/2 teaspoon black pepper, freshly ground

1/2 teaspoon salt

1 tablespoon flour

1 egg, slightly beaten
2 tablespoons fresh cilantro, chopped
1 tablespoon vegetable oil

For the Garam Masala Tomato Curry
1/2 medium onion, peeled and coarsely chopped
2 cloves garlic, peeled and coarsely chopped
1/2 jalapeño chili, seeded and coarsely chopped
1 tablespoon lemon juice
5 plum tomatoes, seeded and chopped (see Cooking Notes, page 27)
1 tablespoon vegetable oil
1/2 teaspoon turmeric
1/2 teaspoon salt
1/4 teaspoon garam masala
3 tablespoons fresh cilantro, chopped

Place the pork in a medium non-metallic bowl. Heat a small skillet over medium-high heat. When hot, add the urad dal and toast until golden brown, 2-3 minutes. Add to the pork bowl. In the same skillet, toast the coriander, cumin and fennel seeds until they release their aroma, about 1-2 minutes. Be careful not to burn! Transfer the spices to the pork bowl. Add the chili, onion, garam masala, black pepper, salt, flour, egg and cilantro to the pork bowl. Using your hands, mix thoroughly, distributing the spices evenly throughout the meat. Form the mixture into small balls, approximately 2 inches in diameter. You should have 16-18 meatballs.

Heat the oil in a large skillet over medium-high heat. Meanwhile place a paper towel on a plate. When the skillet is hot, add the meatballs in batches and brown evenly on all sides, about 10 minutes per batch. Remove the meatballs to the paper towel-lined plate.

To make the tomato curry, purée the onion, garlic, chili and lemon juice in a blender. Remove the purée from the blender and set aside. In the blender, purée the tomatoes. Heat the oil in a large skillet over medium-high heat, add the onion-garlic purée and sauté for 2-3 minutes. Add the tomato purée, turmeric, salt and garam masala, cook 3 minutes. Add the meatballs to the sauce, stir to coat and cook until the sauce begins to bubble. Reduce heat to low, cover and simmer for 10 minutes. Stir in 3/4 cup cold water and continue simmering until the meatballs are fully cooked, another 10-15 minutes. Check the meatballs occasionally and stir to keep them coated with sauce, adding more water if the sauce starts to stick to the pan. The sauce should be thick at the end of the cooking time. Stir in the cilantro and serve.

Raitas & Chutneys

RAITA AUR HERB

*I*NCREDIBLY FRESH AND TASTY, THIS RAITA IS GREAT ON A DIN-
NER OR LUNCH MENU, AND MAKES A TERRIFIC HORS D'OEUVRE
WHEN PAIRED WITH THE FETA CHEESE AND HERB PLATTER (PAGE
24). IF SERVING BOTH THE RAITA AND THE HERB PLATTER, PRE-
PARE THE HERBS FOR THE LATTER RECIPE FIRST AND REMOVE THE
AMOUNTS NEEDED FOR THE RAITA.

YIELDS APPROXIMATELY 2 1/2 CUPS

1/2 long cucumber, peeled and cut into 1/4-inch cubes

1/4 cup raisins or currants

1 1/2 cups lowfat yogurt

3 tablespoons green onion, thinly sliced, including the green tops

12 medium fresh mint leaves, finely chopped

1 tablespoon fresh dill, plucked from stems and finely chopped

1 tablespoon fresh cilantro, coarsely chopped

2 tablespoons blanched slivered almonds, toasted and chopped

2 cloves garlic, peeled and minced

1/2 teaspoon sugar

1/2 teaspoon salt

1/4 teaspoon black pepper, freshly ground

Garnish: 1 tablespoon blanched slivered almonds, toasted

In a bowl, combine all the ingredients except the garnish. Mix well, check
for seasoning and chill. Serve garnished with the almonds.

SABZI WALA RAITA

❋

*R*AITA IS COMMONLY SERVED WITH INDIAN MEALS. IT COOLS THE PALATE AND SERVES AS A FLAVOR COMPLEMENT TO THE OVERALL ARRAY OF DISHES. IN FACT, A MENU IS NOT COMPLETE WITHOUT A VERSION OF THIS YOGURT SALAD.

YIELDS 1 1/2 CUPS

1 cup lowfat yogurt

1 plum tomato, seeded and diced (reserve a sprinkling for garnish)

1/2 cucumber, peeled and diced

1 tablespoon fresh cilantro, coarsely chopped (reserve a sprinkling for garnish)

1/4 teaspoon cumin, toasted and ground

3/4 teaspoon sugar

1/2 teaspoon vegetable oil

1/4 teaspoon brown mustard seeds

1/8 teaspoon salt, or to taste

Freshly ground black pepper, to taste

Mix the yogurt, tomato, cucumber, cilantro, cumin and sugar in a medium bowl. Heat the oil in a small skillet over medium-high heat. When hot, add the mustard seeds and let them pop, about 30 seconds. Stir the oil and the mustard seeds into the yogurt mixture. Add the salt and black pepper to taste. Transfer to a serving bowl, garnish with the reserved tomato and cilantro and serve.

M E E T H I   C H U T N E Y

*T*HIS CHUTNEY HAS A PIQUANT, SWEET FLAVOR AND EXCELLENT
COLOR, MAKING IT A TERRIFIC ACCOMPANIMENT TO MEATS AND
POULTRY OF ANY KIND.

Y I E L D S   A P P R O X I M A T E L Y   2   C U P S

2 tablespoons vegetable oil

1/2 teaspoon panch phoran (see page 18)

3 dried hot red chilies, seeds removed

1 teaspoon turmeric

2 tablespoons sugar

2 large ripe mangoes, peeled and sliced into 1/4-inch thick pieces

5 tablespoons shredded sweetened coconut

1/4 teaspoon salt

2 tablespoons fresh cilantro, coarsely chopped

Heat the oil in a saucepan over medium-high heat. When hot, add the panch
phoran and chilies. Allow the seeds to sputter and the chilies to darken. Be
careful not to burn. Add the turmeric, 1 cup cold water and the sugar. Stir
a couple of times and add the mangoes, coconut and salt. Stir to mix and
bring to a boil. Turn the heat to low and simmer until the mixture thickens
slightly, about 15-20 minutes. Remove from heat, stir in the cilantro and
serve hot with the rest of the meal.

Fresh Mint & Parsley Chutney

THIS CHUTNEY IS EXCELLENT WITH STARCHY VEGETABLES AND FISH, SUCH AS THE BROILED HALIBUT WITH GARAM MASALA (PAGE 76). MIX AND MATCH AS YOU PLEASE. THE CHUTNEY WILL KEEP FOR A WEEK REFRIGERATED, BUT IT IS DEFINITELY MORE APPEALING IN COLOR AFTER THE INITIAL PREPARATION.

YIELDS 1/2 CUP

2 1/2 cups loosely packed fresh mint leaves, coarsely chopped

1 cup fresh parsley, coarsely chopped

A 1 1/2-inch piece fresh ginger, peeled and coarsely chopped

3 cloves garlic, peeled and coarsely chopped

1/4-1/2 jalapeño chili, minced

5 teaspoons tamarind paste (see page 19)

1/2 teaspoon salt

3/4 teaspoon sugar

2 tablespoons lemon juice

Put all of the ingredients into a blender with 2 tablespoons of cold water. Purée the mixture, stopping as you go to scrape the sides with a spatula and push the mixture down to the blades. Transfer to a bowl and serve.

Tamarind Ginger Chutney

IMLI AUR AADRAK

TAMARIND IS AN ANCIENT INGREDIENT STILL USED IN MUCH OF THE WORLD'S GREAT CUISINES. THIS VERSATILE CHUTNEY RECIPE WORKS WELL AS AN ACCOMPANIMENT TO AN INDIAN MEAL OR AS A MARINADE FOR MEATS AND VEGETABLES.

YIELDS 3/4 CUP

1 recipe tamarind paste (see page 19)

1 1/2 teaspoons coriander, toasted and ground

A 2-inch piece fresh ginger, peeled and minced or grated

3/4 teaspoon salt

1/8 teaspoon cayenne

3-5 tablespoons sugar, to taste

Optional: 4 tablespoons golden raisins

In a bowl, combine the tamarind paste with the other ingredients. Mix well to dissolve the sugar and chill. Transfer to a small bowl and serve with other components of a meal.

Tamarind Ginger Chutney with Kalonji & Tart Apples

IMLI CHUTNEY

THIS SWEET AND SOUR CHUTNEY IS A TERRIFIC ACCOMPANIMENT TO AN INDIAN MEAL. TRY IT WITH GOAN SPICED DUCK (PAGE 91).

YIELDS 2 CUPS

1 tablespoon vegetable oil

1 teaspoon kalonji seeds

1 teaspoon brown mustard seeds

1/2 medium onion, peeled and coarsely chopped

1 jalapeño chili, seeded and finely chopped

A 1-inch piece fresh ginger, peeled and minced or grated

1/2 teaspoon coriander, toasted and ground

1/4 teaspoon turmeric

2 tart green apples (Granny Smith or Pippin), cored, peeled and coarsely chopped

1/4 cup golden raisins

1 1/2 tablespoons brown sugar, crumbled

1/2 recipe tamarind paste (see page 19)

1 tablespoon lemon juice

1 teaspoon salt

Heat the oil in a large skillet over medium-high heat. When hot, add the kalonji and mustard seeds, let the seeds pop. Add the onion, chili and ginger. Stir and cook until the onion softens but is not brown, about 3-5 minutes. Add the coriander, turmeric, apples, raisins, brown sugar and 1 cup cold water. Bring to a boil, reduce the heat to low, cover and simmer until the apples are soft and the mixture has thickened, about 20 minutes. Set aside to cool. Add the tamarind paste, lemon juice and salt to the cooked apple mixture, stir to mix well. Chill before serving.

Hot Tomato Chutney

TIMATAR CHUTNEY

THIS MIXTURE IS REALLY MORE OF A SAUCE AND WAS DESIGNED SPECIFICALLY TO GO WITH THE SPICY SPLIT PEA CAKE (PAGE 37) AND EGGPLANT STUFFED WITH AJWAINI SPINACH AND COUSCOUS (PAGE 60). HOWEVER, THE SAUCE IS QUITE VERSATILE AND CAN BE PAIRED WITH MANY DISHES.

YIELDS 2 CUPS

2 teaspoons ghee (see page 19)

1/2 teaspoon cumin seeds

1 small onion, peeled and coarsely chopped

5 plum tomatoes, seeded and coarsely chopped (see Cooking Notes, page 27)

1 tablespoon lemon juice

1/4 teaspoon salt, or to taste

A large pinch black pepper, freshly ground

2 tablespoons fresh cilantro, coarsely chopped

In a medium skillet, heat the ghee over medium-high heat. When hot, add the cumin seeds and let them sizzle for 30 seconds. Reduce the heat to medium and add the onion. Sauté until the onion just begins to brown, about 4 minutes. Add the tomatoes and cook for 5 more minutes.

Place the mixture in a blender. Add the remaining ingredients and purée. Reheat later if necessary, and serve.

Desserts & Drinks

Baked Green Apples with Cardamom

CARDAMOM IS SOMETIMES REFERRED TO AS THE VANILLA OF
INDIA. TO INDIANS, OUR VANILLA IS THE CARDAMOM OF THE
AMERICAS. CARDAMOM IS TERRIFIC IN ALL KINDS OF DESSERTS,
YOGURT DRINKS AND SAVORY MEAT DISHES TOO.

S E R V E S   6

6 tart green apples (Granny Smith or Pippin), cored

6 tablespoons brown sugar, crumbled

2 tablespoons ghee (see page 19) or butter, softened

1/8 teaspoon salt

6 tablespoons blanched slivered almonds, finely chopped

3/8 teaspoon cardamom, removed from pods and ground

1 1/2 lemons, quartered

6-9 tablespoons cream

Garnish: 6 tablespoons blanched slivered almonds, toasted and 6 fresh mint sprigs

Preheat the oven to 375°F and choose a baking dish large enough to comfortably hold all the apples. Trim away about 1/2 inch of the peel from
around the top of each apple where it has been cored. In a small bowl, mix
the crumbled brown sugar, ghee, salt, chopped almonds and cardamom with
your fingers until well combined. Stuff equal parts of the mixture into the
center of each apple. Place the stuffed apples in the baking dish and add 1
cup cold water. Squeeze the juice from the lemon wedges over the top of
each apple. Bake the apples until they soften and are fork-tender, about 45-
50 minutes, basting the apple tops every 15 minutes with the juice from the
baking dish.

Remove the baking dish from the oven and transfer the apples to dessert plates or bowls. Transfer the juice from the bottom of the baking dish to a small skillet. Heat over medium-high heat and reduce until it is caramelized, about 15 minutes. It will become a golden-colored syrup. Spoon a tablespoon of cream and a little of the syrup on top of each apple. Garnish the tops with toasted almonds and mint sprigs. Serve.

Note: This recipe yields about 2 teaspoons of caramel per apple. If more is desired, follow the recipe for the caramel in Orange Custard Scented with Black Cumin (page 118).

♦

Snacks are sold roadside all over India.
This man, with his magnanimous smile, lives
in the beautiful lake city of Udaipur.
He is scooping a tasty selection of fried
garbanzo strands.

♦

Mango Caramel

THIS RECIPE IS MODELED AFTER A SWEET THAT IS SERVED AT THE FAMOUS KARAVALLI RESTAURANT IN BANGALORE. THE MIXTURE CAN BE REDUCED TO A SOFT CANDY, OR COOKED INTO A THICK PURÉE, CHILLED AND SERVED OVER ICE CREAM. THE MANGO PIECES CAN ALSO BE DIPPED IN DARK CHOCOLATE, OR SERVED WITH FRESH STRAWBERRIES, RASPBERRIES OR BLACKBERRIES.

SERVES 8 ♦ 1 PIECE EACH

2 medium mangoes (about 1 1/2 pounds), peeled and cut into slices

2 tablespoons sugar

4 tablespoon corn syrup

1/8 teaspoon cardamom, removed from pods and ground

4 tablespoons ghee (see page 19)

2 tablespoons cream

Garnish: Fresh mint sprigs

In a saucepan, combine the mangoes, sugar, 1 tablespoon of the corn syrup and 3/4 cup cold water. Stir to mix and bring to a boil over medium-high heat. Turn the heat to low and simmer for 20 minutes. Remove the pan from the heat and set aside to cool slightly.

Place the mango mixture in a blender, add the cardamom and purée. Pulse the blender occasionally (turning it off and on again) and scrape the pulp from the sides to catch any remaining mango lumps. The mixture should be about 1 3/4 to 2 cups. If it is less, cut the remaining ingredients proportionately.

In a large, non-stick, thick-sided saucepan, melt the ghee over medium-high heat. When the ghee is hot, add the mango purée, stir and reduce the heat to low. Add the remaining corn syrup and the cream, stir for several minutes to mix well. Fresh mangoes vary in sweetness, so you will have to taste and adjust the sugar if the mixture is bland. Add from 1 to 3 teaspoons of sugar, keeping in mind that the caramel will become sweeter after it is finished. Continue to cook, allowing the mixture to bubble, for 25-30 minutes, stirring occasionally in the beginning and constantly after the mixture has thickened near the end. When the mixture has darkened and begins to form a mass, remove from the heat. (Note: if making the mango purée ice cream topping, remove the pot from the heat after 15 minutes. The mixture should be the consistency of jam.)

Place a 1 1/2-foot piece of plastic wrap onto a cutting board. Spoon the mango mixture in a column along the center of the plastic wrap. Create a seam by bringing the long sides together above the caramel and rolling down to the surface. The caramel will be the shape of a flattened log, about 2 inches wide and 8 inches long. Bring the ends together and tie to secure them. Place the mango caramel in the refrigerator on a flat surface and chill for several hours until firm.

Remove the mango caramel to a cutting board. Untie the ends and face the long rolled seam down. Cut 1-inch wide pieces through the top of the plastic wrap. Undo the plastic from the back and roll the caramel out of the wrap. Serve each piece on a plate garnished with a sprig of fresh mint.

NARANGI CUSTARD AUR SHAHI JEERA

CITRUS, COMPLEMENTED BY THE EXOTIC FLAVOR OF BLACK CUMIN, IS THE PERFECT FINALE FOR A FLAVORFUL INDIAN MEAL. THIS CUSTARD CAN BE A SIMPLE DESSERT ON ITS OWN, OR AN ELEGANT PRESENTATION WITH THE ADDITION OF THE ORANGE CARAMEL TOPPING AND A MINT SPRIG.

SERVES 8

For the Orange Caramel Topping
3 oranges, peeled (peels reserved) and cut into segments (see Cooking Notes, page 29)
1/4 cup brandy
2 teaspoons brown sugar, well crumbled
1 cup sugar

For the Custard
2 large eggs
6 large egg yolks
1/2 cup sugar
A pinch salt
1 cup milk (Note: Do not use lowfat or nonfat milk)
3 cups cream
Peel of 2 oranges, reserved from Orange Caramel Topping
1/4 teaspoon black cumin, toasted

Eight 6-ounce ramekins

Garnish: Fresh mint sprigs

Preheat the oven to 325°F. Place the orange segments in a shallow bowl. Pour the brandy over the oranges and sprinkle with the brown sugar. Set aside.

To make the caramel, combine the sugar and 1/2 cup plus 3 tablespoons cold water in a medium saucepan. Cook over medium heat, swirling the pan occasionally, until it is an amber color, about 10-15 minutes. Remove from the heat. Stir 3 tablespoons of the caramel into the orange segments and refrigerate. Pour the remaining caramel into the bottoms of the ramekins. Set the ramekins aside to cool.

To make the custard, combine the eggs, egg yolks, sugar and salt in a large mixing bowl. Whisk to combine and set aside. Pour the milk and cream into a medium saucepan. Add the orange peel and black cumin and bring to a boil over high heat. Immediately remove the milk mixture from the heat and slowly whisk it into the egg yolk mixture. Refrigerate the custard until cool, and then strain through a sieve to remove the orange peels.

Pour the custard into the caramel-lined ramekins and place the ramekins in an oven-proof pan. Place the pan in the oven and pour hot water into the pan until it reaches 2 inches up the ramekin sides. Bake the custard until the centers feel barely firm, about 50-60 minutes. Refrigerate for 4 hours or overnight.

When ready to serve, run a knife along the edge of each ramekin and unmold onto a plate. Heat the orange caramel until it melts and the orange segments break apart slightly. Top each custard with the orange caramel topping and garnish with a mint sprig.

Lemon, Ginger & Mint Drink

PANNA

❀❀❀

THIS REFRESHING DRINK COMPLEMENTS THE COMPLEX FLAVORS OF INDIAN DISHES. IT CAN ALSO BE USED AS A SORT OF SPORT DRINK AFTER EXERCISE OR A HOT SAUNA.

SERVES 6

1/4 cup sugar

A 3-inch piece fresh ginger, peeled and thinly sliced

2 lemons, sliced crosswise (reserve 6 slices for garnish)

8 slices cucumber, peeled and cut 1/4 inch thick

6 sprigs fresh mint, plus garnish

In a small saucepan, combine 1/2 cup cold water and the sugar, heat over medium-high and stir until the sugar is dissolved. Add the ginger slices and bring to a boil. Turn the heat to low and simmer for 15 minutes. Do not let the syrup become too thick.

While the ginger syrup is simmering, put the lemon slices, cucumber slices and mint sprigs in a 2-quart pitcher and stir to bruise with a wooden spoon. Fill the pitcher with water. When the syrup is ready, quickly stir it into the pitcher.

Serve in tall glasses over ice, garnished with lemon slices and mint sprigs.

AARU LASSI

A PUZZLING QUESTION OFTEN ASKED IS, "WHAT TYPE OF WINE SHOULD BE SERVED WITH INDIAN FOOD?" UNFORTUNATELY, WINE IS NOT THE GREATEST BEVERAGE TO PAIR WITH SPICY, COMPLEX FOOD. IF AN ALCOHOLIC BEVERAGE IS A MUST, THE SWEETER ASIAN BEERS ARE THE BEST CHOICE. HOWEVER, YOGURT LASSIS OR ICE WATER ARE THE BEVERAGES TRADITIONALLY SERVED WITH INDIAN CUISINE. YOGURT HAS A COOLING EFFECT ON THE PALATE, AND THERE IS NOTHING MORE REFRESHING TO ACCOMPANY THE EARTHY FLAVOR OF HOT SPICY FOODS. BY THE WAY, A LASSI IS NOT SYNONYMOUS WITH OUR YOGURT SMOOTHIE. THE THIN CONSISTENCY OF THE LASSI IS LESS FILLING AND MORE APPROPRIATE FOR A DINNER DRINK.

SERVES 4 ♦ 1 CUP EACH

2 fresh peaches (about 1/2 pound), peeled and sliced,
or 1/2 of a 16-ounce can sliced peaches

2 cups nonfat or lowfat yogurt

A large pinch cardamom, removed from pods and ground

2 teaspoons fresh mint leaves, finely chopped

2-4 tablespoons sugar

10 ice cubes

Put all of the ingredients into a blender. If using canned peaches, include half the syrup from the can. Purée, pulsing if necessary to break up the ice cubes. Serve cold.

Spiced Milk Tea

THE SPICED TEA OF INDIA PROVIDES A WARM AND SATISFYING END TO A FLAVORFUL MEAL. WHEN NO ONE FEELS LIKE DESSERT, THIS TEA OFFERS THE PERFECT, SLIGHTLY SWEET FINISH, AND THE GINGER PROVIDES A PLEASANT BIT OF HEAT THAT ANY INDIAN NATIVE WILL TELL YOU AIDS THE DIGESTION.

SERVES 4

1/2 cup lowfat milk

A 3-inch stick cinnamon

A 1/2-inch piece fresh ginger, peeled and minced or grated

2 whole cloves

4 green cardamom pods, slightly crushed

1/4 teaspoon black peppercorns

4-6 teaspoons sugar, or to taste

2 tablespoons loose tea, or 4 tea bags, black, orange pekoe or Darjeeling variety

In a large saucepan, combine 5 cups cold water, the milk, spices and sugar. Stir and bring to a boil. Remove from the heat and let the spices permeate the liquid for 5-10 minutes, or longer if you have the time. Add the tea and bring the mixture to a boil for a second time. Reduce the heat to low and simmer for 5 minutes. Check for flavor and add more sugar, milk, tea or even water according to your taste. Carefully pour or strain the tea, leaving the spices behind. Serve hot.

Sample Menus

❧

*T*he recipes you choose for a meal should fit the occasion. Use the listed menus as a starting point for learning how to plan an Indian meal. When cooking for a large number of people, it is fun to prepare many different dishes. Each person's plate becomes a dazzling array of color and texture—the effect always impresses guests. For a small meal, create a nice balance of flavor with just a few dishes. For instance, if you choose one yogurt dish, offset it with a dish that is more tangy than creamy. ♦ All the recipes give a range of green chili or cayenne to use. This feature allows you to control the heat of each dish for balance within a menu. Choose which dishes to scale up in heat and leave others in the more mild range. In this manner, flavor, heat, spice and aroma will all combine to create a satisfying meal. ♦ If you do decide to prepare a large meal, remember "an ounce of prevention is worth a pound of cure." In other words, plan a few days in advance and prepare everything possible: soak the beans, even cook the meat, as it absorbs flavor over time. But wait to prepare the vegetable and fish dishes until the day of the party.

A Delightful Weekend Lunch or Dinner

Suraj Turkey Kebabs (page 93)
Roasted Okra with Amchoor and Tomatoes (page 62)
Bengali Mango Chutney (page 108)
Lentils with Panch Phoran (page 48)
Aromatic Basmati Rice (page 40)
Lemon, Ginger and Mint Drink (page 120)

For the Barbecue

Cabbage Salad with Chili and Cumin Dressing (page 26)
Tandoori-Style Chicken (page 90)
Prawns Spiced with Fenugreek Seeds and Lime (page 78)
Creamy Roasted Eggplant with Shahi Masala (page 58)
Fresh Mint and Parsley Chutney (page 109)
Herbed Raita (page 106)

Dinner for More than One Night — for People on the Move

Radish Lentil Soup (page 30)
Spiced Ground Beef with Peas and Carrots (page 96)
Garden Vegetable Raita with Brown Mustard Seeds (page 107)
Tamarind Ginger Chutney (page 110)
Basmati Rice with Lima Beans and Currants (page 42)

A Supper for Guests

Semolina Crab Crêpes with Red Pepper Sauce (page 34)
Broiled Halibut with Garam Masala and Mint Chutney (page 76)
Spicy Potatoes with Amchoor and Dill (page 66)
Herbed Raita (page 106)
Indian Flat Breads (page 49)
Baked Green Apples with Cardamom (page 114)

A Royal Feast – Served as a Buffet after a Seated Soup Course

Feta Cheese and Herb Platter (page 24)
Spinach, Sweet Corn and Cilantro Soup (page 32)
Braised Cauliflower with Panch Phoran Yogurt Sauce (page 56)
Roasted Butternut Squash with Ajwain and Cashews (page 72)
Sautéed Prawns in Spiced Yogurt (page 80)
Lamb Scented with Cinnamon, Cilantro and Mint (page 100)
Basmati Rice with Green Onion and Dill (page 41)
Bengali Mango Chutney (page 108)
Orange Custard Scented with Black Cumin (page 118)

A Vegetarian Brahmin Feast – Served as a Buffet

Eggplant Stuffed with Ajwaini Spinach and Couscous (page 60)
Green Beans with Mustard Seeds and Almonds (page 52)
Potatoes with Garam Masala and Spicy Tomato (page 68)
Lentils with Panch Phoran (page 48)
Garden Vegetable Raita with Brown Mustard Seeds (page 107)
Aromatic Basmati Rice (page 40)
Tamarind Ginger Chutney (page 110)
Mango Caramel (page 116)
Spiced Milk Tea (page 122)

Index